LIFE|EXPLORED

WHAT'S THE BEST GIFT
GOD COULD GIVE YOU?

LEADER'S HANDBOOK

Life Explored Leader's Handbook
Copyright © 2016 Christianity Explored
www.explo.red

Published by:
The Good Book Company Ltd
Blenheim House, 1 Blenheim Road, Epsom, Surrey, KT19 9AP, UK
Tel: 0333 123 0880; International: +44 (0) 208 942 0880
Email: info@thegoodbook.co.uk

Websites:
UK and Europe: www.thegoodbook.co.uk
North America: www.thegoodbook.com
Australia: www.thegoodbook.com.au
New Zealand: www.thegoodbook.co.nz

ISBN: 9781784980832

Design by André Parker

Printed in India

WELCOME TO

LIFE|**EXPLORED**

What's the best gift God could give you?

What we desire most in life determines our dispositions, our decisions, and ultimately, our destinies. Over seven sessions, *Life Explored* helps people uncover what they're really living for, and shows how, in Christ, God meets our deepest desire for happiness.

Our hope and prayer is not just that people will have a wonderful experience of *Life Explored*, and not just that they will come to know the Bible better. One of life's greatest tragedies is that many who know their Bibles back to front do not know its Author. Our hope and prayer is that people will begin to experience God, because no happiness in life is higher, no pleasure is deeper, and no gift could be more wonderful.

"The Bible is not an end in itself," wrote the evangelist A. W. Tozer, "but a means to bring people to an intimate and satisfying knowledge of God, that they may enter into him, that they may delight in his presence, may taste and know the inner sweetness of the very God himself in the core and centre of their hearts."

What's the best gift God could give you? Himself.

The Life Explored Team

CONTENTS

SECTION 1
HOW TO RUN LIFE EXPLORED

life.explo.red
is the official website for *Life Explored*, featuring content for both guests and leaders.

Register your course and you'll receive an exclusive web address where you and your guests can watch any of the films, at any time.

GETTING
STARTED

What's the big theme of *Life Explored*?

We all want to be happy. Why is lasting happiness so hard to find?

Life Explored is an exposé of the little gods that promise us so much happiness, yet deliver so little. As it explores the Bible story (creation, fall, redemption, new creation), *Life Explored* shows how our deepest desires for happiness can only be satisfied in one person. The best gift God can give us is himself.

Who's it intended for?

Life Explored has been designed to speak powerfully to those who don't consider themselves to be religious and have never read the Bible. But it will also stimulate good discussions among followers of Christ, too.

What's the structure of *Life Explored*?

Life Explored is made up of seven sessions. Each session works like this:

- **Film 1** | 10 minutes
- **Discussion 1** | 5 minutes
- **Bible Reading** | 2 minutes
- **Film 2** | 15 minutes
- **Bible Reading** | 3 minutes
- **Discussion 2** | 25 minutes

If you have longer than an hour, give yourself more time to complete Discussion 2. Although you should be able to complete Discussion 2 in 25 minutes, you'll benefit from having an extra 15-20 minutes, especially if your group is larger than a few people.

What's the aim of Film 1?

The first films are not intended to be retellings of biblical stories. They are their own stories, and help to create a "Nathan moment".

In 2 Samuel 12, Nathan was the prophet who confronted David about his murder and adultery.

But remember how Nathan does it. Rather than immediately saying, "You've sinned grievously against the Lord! Repent!", Nathan takes a very different, and very effective, approach. He tells David a story. The story provokes powerful emotions in David: sympathy towards the innocent character in the story, and anger towards the guilty character.

After the story is told, Nathan says to David, *That character you're so angry about? That's you. You are the man!* (2 Samuel 12:7). Immediately, David is struck to the core and driven to repent – because the story has allowed him to see his actions from a different perspective.

That's the combined aim of the two films. The first tells a story which hopefully enables the viewer to see things from a different perspective. The second film uses that story to bring biblical truth home to the viewer's heart.

What's the aim of Discussion 1?

The first discussion is prompted by a single diagnostic question.

For example: "Sometimes we feel our lives would be happier 'if only' we had someone or something. What's your 'if only'?"

Or: "What, if you lost it, would make you feel that life wasn't worth living?"

Listen carefully to the answers given, and you should be able to get a handle on the "god(s)" people are living for. That can be a helpful pointer for your one-to-one conversations with each person, as you seek to show how Christ is infinitely better than the gods we love and serve instead.

What's the connection between Film 1 and Discussion 1?

In each session, Film 1 helps to create a "Nathan moment" (see above) that leads into the opening discussion question.

1. **Overture** | A preview of the six stories we'll be experiencing together on *Life Explored*, and an introduction to the opening question: **What's the best gift God could give you?**

2. **Hotel** | Colonial India. A girl's view of her best friend is changed unexpectedly, and forever. **What's your current view of God, and how did you reach that viewpoint?**

3. **Gold** | The Californian gold rush. A prospector risks his life in the quest for gold. **What keeps you going in difficult situations?**

4. **Lawn** | Suburbia. A man is hooked by a late night infomercial and feels his life would be complete if only he could have the perfect garden. **What's your "if only"?**

5. **Geisha** | Edo-Period Japan. A woman is drawn away from her husband and family in pursuit of what she hopes will be a more exciting life. **What are you hoping will bring you fulfilment in life?**

6. **Celebrity** | Los Angeles. A Hollywood actress has everything, but something isn't right. **What, if you lost it, would make you feel that life wasn't worth living?**

7. **Space** | In orbit above the earth. As his space station disintegrates around him, an astronaut reflects on his life. **What's the best gift God could give you?**

	△ Film 1	≡ Discussion 1	△ Film 2	≡ Discussion 2
Session 1 **The Good God**	Overture Part 1	What's the best gift God could give you?	Overture Part 2 **Genesis 1**	Psalm 19
Session 2 **The Trustworthy God**	Hotel Part 1	What's your current view of God, and how did you reach that viewpoint?	Hotel Part 2 **Genesis 2-3**	Romans 1
Session 3 **The Generous God**	Gold Part 1	What keeps you going in difficult situations?	Gold Part 2 **Genesis 12**	Luke 19
Session 4 **The Liberating God**	Lawn Part 1	Often we feel our lives would be happier "if only" we had someone or something. What's your "if only"?	Lawn Part 2 **Exodus 12**	Matthew 11

SECTION 1 | **HOW TO RUN LIFE EXPLORED**

	▷ Film 1	≡ Discussion 1	▷ Film 2	≡ Discussion 2
Session 5 **The Fulfilling God**	Geisha Part 1	What are you hoping will bring you fulfilment in life?	Geisha Part 2 **John 4**	Luke 15
Session 6 **The Life-Giving God**	Celebrity Part 1	What, if you lost it, would make you feel that life wasn't worth living?	Celebrity Part 2 **1 Corinthians 15**	Acts 17
Session 7 **The Joyful God**	Space Part 1	What's the best gift God could give you?	Space Part 2 **Revelation 21-22**	Matthew 22

13

What's the aim of Film 2?

The second film presents teaching which aims to contrast the God of the Bible with the "gods" we give our lives to instead. We explore our yearning desire for happiness, and show how that desire is finally met in Jesus Christ.

What's the aim of Discussion 2?

Discussion 2 is an opportunity to explore a Bible passage together. Each passage has been chosen to complement the main theme for that session.

How should I start each session?

It's a good idea to invite people to arrive about 30 minutes before the session officially starts. That gives you time to share food or coffee first so people can get to know each other. It also helps you start your session on time.

How should I end each session?

At the end of each session, thank your guest(s) for coming, but make it clear that they're very welcome to stay around if they'd like to. Some of the best conversations will happen over a cup of coffee once the session has ended.

A guest's answer to the last question ("What has been most striking for you during this session?") gives you a great launchpad for further conversation, once the session is officially over.

What's the best way to prepare for *Life Explored*?

1. Pray! And keep praying throughout the course.

2. Prepare for the "big seven" tough questions (see pages 25-26).

3. See the note on page 23 on "How can I encourage people to come?"

4. Register your course (at www.life.explo.red). That will give you access to training modules designed especially for *Life Explored* leaders.

GOD'S ROLE IN EVANGELISM
AND OURS

As we lead *Life Explored*, we need to distinguish between God's role in evangelism and our role. It's going to be frustrating if we try to fulfil God's role – because only the Creator of the universe is able to do that.

Read 2 Corinthians 4:1-6

Answer the following questions from the verses you've just read:

What is God's role in evangelism?

Why can't people see the truth of the gospel?

What is our role in evangelism?

How should we carry out our role in evangelism?

God's role in evangelism

God makes "his light shine in our hearts to give us the light of the knowledge of God's glory displayed in the face of Christ" (2 Corinthians 4:6).

In other words, God enables us to recognize that Jesus is God. God makes it possible – by his Holy Spirit – for a person to see who Jesus is. When Paul is on the Damascus road, he asks, "Who are you, Lord?" and is told, "I am Jesus" (Acts 9:5). That is the moment of his conversion – when he recognizes for the first time who Jesus actually is.

The beginning of 2 Corinthians 4:6 reminds us that God said, "Let light shine out of darkness". That is a reference to the miracle of creation in Genesis 1:3. This same God who brought light into the world at creation now shines light into the hearts of human beings, enabling them to see that Jesus is God. In other words, for people to recognize that Jesus is God, God must perform a miracle.

People do not become Christians just because we share the gospel with them. God must shine his light in people's hearts so that they recognize and respond to the truth of the gospel.

And we know from 2 Corinthians 4:4 that people can't see the truth of the gospel because "the god of this age has blinded the minds of unbelievers".

The "god of this age", as befits his name, wants people to be preoccupied only with this age. Our popularity, our families, our relationships, our material possessions. It is not that these are bad in themselves. But they become bad when they blind us to anything beyond them.

When that happens, we see Jesus only as a man – perhaps as a great moral teacher or social worker or healer. We're blinded to his divine identity. According to verse 4, that's because Satan is determined to prevent people from seeing "the light of the gospel that displays the glory of Christ, who is the image of God." He does not want people to recognize who Jesus is.

Our role in evangelism

What then is our role in evangelism? "We preach ... Jesus Christ as Lord" (verse 5).

The word "preach" can evoke negative images, but it derives from a word simply meaning "herald": someone who relates important announcements from the king to his kingdom. Our role is to tell people the gospel and pray that the Spirit of God will convict them of its truth.

These verses also reveal the attitude we should adopt as we preach. We are to be like "servants for Jesus' sake" (2 Corinthians 4:5). The word translated "servants" literally means "slaves" in Greek. Paul was determined to present Christ to others without any hint of self-promotion.

One pastor tells the story of a church visitor who greeted him with the words, "So, you're the man who has all the answers!" His response was, "No, I'm just a man pointing to the one who does". That's the humble spirit of 2 Corinthians 4:5.

We must remember that the only difference between ourselves and an unbeliever is that God, in his grace, has opened our blind eyes and illuminated our hearts by his Holy Spirit (verse 6). We should be forever grateful, and so seek to promote Christ, not ourselves.

We must keep preaching Christ as Lord and, remembering that only a miracle from God can open blind eyes, we must keep praying that God will shine his light in the hearts of unbelievers.

2 Corinthians 4:1-6 also helps us to carry out our role in the right way: "We do not use deception, nor do we distort the word of God ... By setting forth the truth plainly we commend ourselves to everyone's conscience in the sight of God ... For what we preach is not ourselves, but Jesus Christ as Lord."

That means, when we tell people about Christ, we should be demonstrating:

Integrity – "We do not use deception." We are straight with people; we are genuine and sincere, and we never use any kind of emotional manipulation.

Fidelity – We do not "distort the word of God". We have to tell people the tough bits. If, for example, we don't tell people about sin, about hell, and about the necessity of repentance, then we are distorting God's word. Preaching these hard truths means trusting in the work of the Holy Spirit to draw people to Christ, however "difficult" the message.

Humility – "What we preach is not ourselves, but Jesus Christ as Lord." We must draw people to Jesus, not to ourselves. We want them to follow Christ because they are convinced by the truth and are being led by the Holy Spirit, rather than being manipulated by their admiration of the course leader.

Prepare your personal story

"Always be prepared to give an answer to everyone who asks you to give the reason for the hope that you have. But do this with gentleness and respect..."

1 Peter 3:15

A personal story or testimony is an account of God's work in your life. Everybody who has been born again and who is becoming like Christ has a unique, interesting and powerful story, regardless of whether or not it appears spectacular.

At some point during the course, you may feel it appropriate to share your story with the group. Often someone will ask you directly how you became a Christian and you will need to have an answer ready.

You may find the guidelines below helpful as you prepare your story:

- Keep it honest, personal and interesting.

Tip: Your first sentence should make people sit up and listen. Anything too general – for example, "Well, I was brought up in a Christian home..." – may make people switch off immediately.

- Keep it short.

Tip: Any more than three minutes may stretch people's patience. They can always ask you questions if they want to know more.

- Keep pointing to Christ, not yourself.

Tip: Your story is a great opportunity to communicate the gospel. Always include what it is that you believe, as well as how you came to believe it. As a general guide, try to explain why you think Jesus is God, how his death affects you personally, and what changes God has made in your life.

- Prepare your personal story. (List the main points below.) You might find it useful to share your story with other leaders and get their feedback.

_____

_____

Helping someone who wants to follow Christ

When someone shares with you their desire to follow Christ for the first time, it's surely one of the most joyous privileges of the Christian life.

But like Jesus, we need to be clear – from the outset – about what prospective believers are getting themselves into. In Luke 14, Jesus says, "Whoever does not carry their cross and follow me cannot be my disciple. Suppose one of you wants to build a tower. Won't you first sit down and estimate the cost to see if you have enough money to complete it? For if you lay the foundation and are not able to finish it, everyone who sees it will ridicule you, saying, 'This person began to build and wasn't able to finish.'" (Luke 14:27-30)

Grace may be free, but it is not cheap. It cost Jesus his life. And it will cost us our lives too, if we want to follow him. The invitation may be extended to all, but only those who obey Jesus' call – to carry their cross – can receive it.

So when we find ourselves in the privileged position of helping someone who wants to follow Christ, we must be clear about what following him will mean for them.

And according to Jesus, it means we must "repent and believe" (Mark 1:15). This won't be easy in a world which rejects Jesus and those who want to follow him.

- Explain that "**repent**" means we turn around from the direction we're currently heading in, and turn back to God. We start living life to please him, rather than continuing to rebel against him.

- Explain that "**believe**" means we believe that Jesus is who he says he is, and that he died for our sin on the cross – and we're putting our trust in him as a result.

So to repent and believe is something that we do decisively at a moment in time, but it is not just a moment to look back on; it is a new, ongoing way of life. Help your guest to see what repentance and belief will look like in their daily lives:

- **A new attitude to God.** A follower of Jesus is deeply thankful to God, longs to know him better and love him more. This longing is nurtured by reading the Bible, praying, and spending time with his people.

  Encourage your guest by offering to read the Bible one-to-one with them, and suggesting some daily Bible-reading notes. A follow-up course like *Discipleship Explored* is also a great way for a new believer to get started.

  Encourage them to pray to God about what they've discovered on *Life Explored*, thanking him for Jesus and what he means to them. Assure them that they can speak freely in their own words, because God sees our hearts and understands our deepest longings, even if our words are hesitant and uncertain.

- **A new attitude to God's people.** A follower of Jesus longs to love and serve their Christian brothers and sisters – and, in turn, be loved and served by them.

  This shows itself when a new believer commits themselves to a local church – a particular body of believers they can love. As Jesus said, "Love one another. As I have loved you, so you must love one another. By this everyone will know that you are my disciples, if you love one another" (John 13:34-35).

  Jesus also commanded his followers to be baptized (Matthew 28:18-20) as a way of publicly identifying with Christ and his people. Encourage your guest to speak to their pastor or minister about being baptized.

  Offer to meet your guest at church on Sunday, and help them to establish a pattern of attending each week. Encourage them to join a small group, and to use whatever skills they have in serving their brothers and sisters in Christ.

- **A new attitude to ourselves.** A follower of Jesus longs to please him by rejecting sin, and living for Jesus instead.

  There will be areas of our lives which we know – or will come to see – are not pleasing to Jesus. To repent and believe means that we willingly turn away from those ways of living, and try to live life in the way God intends. This is the life Jesus described as life "to the full" (John 10:10).

- **A new attitude to others.** A follower of Jesus seeks to love others.

  We're called to reflect Christ by relating to others with love, looking for ways to treat them as we would treat ourselves: "So in everything, do to others what you would have them do to you" (Matthew 7:12). And one aspect of that love for others will be our desire to tell them the good news about what Jesus has done.

FAQS

Where should we meet? Wherever works for the people you're inviting. Somewhere warm and welcoming, and where you're able to show the films. If you're meeting in a public place (e.g. a coffee shop), try to find somewhere that isn't too noisy or distracting, and where you won't be disturbed.

How often should we meet? Ideally once a week. Longer than that, and earlier sessions might be forgotten. Shorter than that, and it may feel a little like drinking from a fire hose.

How do I encourage people to come to *Life Explored*? By all means, use posters, banners and postal invitations. You can get hold of personalized publicity from The Good Book Company.

However, by far the most effective way to get people along is one your church may already have in place: friends bringing friends. The whole church family can get involved in this way.

At the risk of stating the obvious, in order to invite non-Christians friends, you're going to need non-Christian friends. Be intentional in the places you spend time and the relationships you cultivate. Share life with people. Love them. And then invite them to come to *Life Explored* with you.

At least six weeks in advance of your course, show the *Life Explored* teaser at your church (available online and on the *Life Explored* DVD). Explain that *Life Explored* has been designed for friends and family who don't yet know Jesus. Share the teaser and short films on social media if you can. Add the hashtag #LifeExplored so we can help promote your course online.

Encourage everyone in your church family to be praying for and inviting people over the coming six weeks, and have invitations available for church members to take away with them.

What happens if someone isn't able to make every session? If someone has to miss a session, they can watch the missed episode online, using their Handbook to complete the session at home.

Register your course online, and you'll be sent a web address where you and your guests can watch any of the films, at any time.

How many leaders should there be on *Life Explored*? The best ratio is no more than three guests to one leader.

Can I run *Life Explored* one to one? Yes, you can. *Life Explored* is completely scaleable.

It can be as intimate as two people watching a film on a phone/tablet/laptop and having a conversation in a coffee shop. Or you can have multiple tables of people in a large venue, watching the films on a projector screen.

Can I give live talks in place of the films?

Yes. For each session, simply discuss the opening question, give a live talk (download talk transcripts from www.life.explo.red), and then finish as usual by exploring the Bible together.

Do I need to give people a Bible?

We've included Bible passages in the *Life Explored* Handbooks. That way, each passage is easy to find, and everyone is focused on the same translation of the text.

But we'd encourage you to give every guest a copy of the Bible, so that they can take it away with them, and explore God's word at their own pace.

What Bible version is Life Explored based on?

Life Explored is based on the New International Version (NIV 2011).

Who should read the Bible passages before Film 2 and Discussion 2?

To avoid making group members feel unnecessarily awkward, we recommend that a leader reads the Bible passages aloud.

(For each session, we've provided a few sentences that should make your transition into the Bible passages seamless.)

How can I answer tough questions?

Each person is fearfully and wonderfully made by God, each with their own story, their own suffering, and their own questions. It's vitally important, then, to be listening carefully, rather than simply waiting for a chance to recite a pre-rehearsed answer.

That said, the "big seven" questions tend to recur frequently (especially the first one), so you should think them through before you begin *Life Explored*:

- **What about evil and suffering?** There can't be a good and powerful God if there's evil and suffering in the world.

- **What about other religions?** There can't be only one true "way".

- **What about my freedom?** If I believe in Christianity, I become a slave because I have to follow the teaching of the Bible / the church.

- **What about hypocrisy in the church?** There are evil and intolerant people who say they're Christians – and many good people who are not Christians – so Christianity can't be true.

- **What about judgment?** The idea that God is angry or judges people goes against the idea that God is loving.

- **What about science?** Science (especially evolutionary theory) has shown that we have no need for God or Christianity.

- **What about the Bible?** It's out of date, full of mistakes, and socially regressive.

It's a very good idea to write out briefly, in advance, how you would engage with those seven objections. We give some brief pointers at the back of this Leader's Handbook (page 85).

Are there any books that will help me answer tough questions? *If You Could Ask God One Question* by Paul Williams and Barry Cooper is a good, entry-level treatment of the questions above.

The Reason for God by Tim Keller is more advanced but still accessible.

Can I Really Trust The Bible? by Barry Cooper is a short book that covers the most frequently asked questions about the Bible itself.

Questioning Evangelism by Randy Newman covers some of the big questions, and offers excellent general advice on how to make conversation with non-Christian friends more fruitful.

What happens if I can't answer someone's question?

It's absolutely fine to tell people that you don't know the answer to a particular question. Ask your guest(s) if it would be ok to discuss it at the next session when you've had time to give it some more thought.

What if someone asks a question that is "off-topic" during the session?

Thank your guest for the question, and explain that for the sake of keeping things "on topic", you'd love to follow it up with them at the end of the session.

It's always tempting to try and answer every question as it comes up, but if you do, there's a good chance that a) you won't have time to complete the session in the limited time you have, and b) other group members may lose interest or focus as the conversation wanders.

Why is the discussion question for Session 1 and 7 the same?

The repeated question is designed to give you a sense of how people's views have changed over the course of seven sessions.

Life Explored talks a lot about happiness. Is that really what the Bible means when it speaks of joy?

We sometimes assume that "happiness" is one thing, and "joy" is another. Usually, happiness is thought to be fleeting and frothy, whereas joy is something that is deeper and longer-lasting.

However, the Bible itself makes no such distinction. In *Life Explored*, we've mostly chosen to use the word "happiness" simply because it is more familiar to people in non-religious contexts.

For more on joy/happiness, see Randy Alcorn's *Happiness*.

Is there a supporting website for Life Explored?

Yes. Visit www.life.explo.red.

Is there a follow-up course for Life Explored?

If your guest isn't yet a follower of Christ, the ideal follow-up course is *Christianity Explored* (based on Mark's Gospel). If they are a follower of Christ, either *Christianity Explored* or *Discipleship Explored* (based on Philippians) is the way to go. Both have been created by the team behind *Life Explored*.

An excellent way to follow up *Life Explored* is to offer to read a book of the Bible "one to one" with your friend. See *One-to-One Bible Reading* by David Helm to get started.

Do I need to have run Christianity Explored to run Life Explored?

You can run *Life Explored* completely independently of *Christianity Explored*.

However, a great way to use the Explored trilogy of courses is to run them in this order:

- *Christianity Explored*
- *Life Explored*
- *Discipleship Explored*

or

- *Life Explored*
- *Christianity Explored*
- *Discipleship Explored*

That way, you could have a rolling, year-long programme running at your church – autumn, spring and summer. *Life Explored* and *Christianity Explored* are ideal for both non-Christians and Christians, and *Discipleship Explored* is intended for those who've become followers of Christ.

How can I get better at telling others about Jesus?

Church-run courses and curricula such as *Life Explored* can be a great way of introducing people to Jesus.

However, they're not a substitute for our own personal evangelism. Some of our friends may never sign up for a course, but they will have regular contact with us. So how can we become better at telling them about Jesus?

We talk most freely and naturally about those things we're most passionate about. As Jesus says in Matthew 12:34, "The mouth speaks what the heart is full of".

If, then, our hearts are full of the beauty of Christ, we will speak about him.

If, on the other hand, our hearts are full of other "gods" (whether they be health, or family, or sex, or money, or the approval of others, or whatever), then we probably won't share the good news about Jesus. And if we do, it's likely to seem forced, half-hearted, or insincere.

The best way, then, to equip ourselves for personal evangelism is to become more passionate about Jesus Christ than anything or anyone else in our lives. God fuels that passion as we pray, meditate on the Bible, and serve our local church.

The more our hearts are filled with him, the more he will overflow into our everyday conversations.

Recommended reading: *Honest Evangelism* by Rico Tice with Carl Laferton; *Questioning Evangelism* by Randy Newman.

Is there any other recommended reading for *Life Explored*?

Idolatry is a central theme of the Bible, and of *Life Explored*.

Tim Keller's book *Counterfeit Gods* is an excellent, readable introduction to the subject. It's ideal for non-Christian readers too.

A more detailed and technical work is *We Become What We Worship* by Greg Beale. This is a biblical theology of idolatry, which aims to trace the theme as it appears throughout Scripture.

SECTION 2
LIFE EXPLORED SESSIONS

INTRODUCTION

This section contains each of the seven sessions you'll be exploring with your guest(s). It includes all the material in their Handbook, plus additional notes and answers intended for leaders.

- If anyone misses a session, bring them up to speed before you start. The talk summaries will help you do this. (If you've registered your course at **www.life.explo.red**, you and your guests will also have online access to the films – ideal for catching up on missed sessions.)

- Some guests may feel that the Bible isn't reliable as a source of history. That's a great question to raise, but can take a while to answer well. Either discuss it one to one at the end of the session, or recommend a book such as *Can I Really Trust The Bible?* by Barry Cooper.

Key

▷ Show a film

💬 Discuss a question

📖 Read a Bible passage

SESSION 1
THE GOOD GOD

▷ **Overture Part 1** (3 min 50 sec)

≡ **What's the best gift God could give you?**
(5 minutes, page 7 of Handbook.)

Note: You may want to write down people's answers, either now or later, as you'll be returning to this question in Session 7.

📖 **We're going to watch the next film now. By way of introduction, let me read you a little bit of Genesis chapter 1.** (Page 8 of Handbook.)

²⁷ God created mankind in his own image,
 in the image of God he created them;
 male and female he created them.

²⁸ God blessed them and said to them, "Be fruitful and increase in number; fill the earth and subdue it. Rule over the fish in the sea and the birds in the sky and over every living creature that moves on the ground."

²⁹ Then God said, "I give you every seed-bearing plant on the face of the whole earth and every tree that has fruit with seed in it. They will be yours for food. ³⁰ And to all the beasts of the earth and all the birds in the sky and all the creatures that move along the ground – everything that has the breath of life in it – I give every green plant for food." And it was so.

³¹ God saw all that he had made, and it was very good.
Genesis 1:27-31

Blessed | Looked on them with love and promised good things.

Subdue | Bring order to.

▷ **Overture Part 2** (11 min 02 sec)

Note: The following talk summary is on page 9 of the Handbook.

• Human beings have been described as "the glory and the garbage" of the universe.

• We're "glorious" because we're made by a glorious God, who has made us "in his own image" (Genesis 1:27).

• Being made "in God's image" means that we can know and enjoy this God. God wants us to enjoy him!

• We flourish most, and enjoy him best, when we reflect him best.

• But there's the "garbage" too. Rather than enjoying and reflecting our Creator, we enjoy and reflect "created things" more. We have other "gods".

• A person's "god" is anything they cling to and rely upon for their ultimate security and contentment.

📖 **Everyone seeks happiness. But are we searching in the right place? We're going to look at a part of the Bible that explores that question – Psalm 19.** (Page 10 of Handbook.)

¹ The heavens declare the glory of God;
the skies proclaim the work of his hands.
² Day after day they pour forth speech;
night after night they reveal knowledge.

³ They have no speech, they use no words;
    no sound is heard from them.
⁴ Yet their voice goes out into all the earth,
    their words to the ends of the world.
    In the heavens God has pitched a tent for the sun.
⁵ It is like a bridegroom coming out of his chamber,
    like a champion rejoicing to run his course.
⁶ It rises at one end of the heavens
    and makes its circuit to the other;
    nothing is deprived of its warmth.

⁷ The law of the LORD is perfect,
    refreshing the soul.
The statutes of the LORD are trustworthy,
    making wise the simple.
⁸ The precepts of the LORD are right,
    giving joy to the heart.
The commands of the LORD are radiant,
    giving light to the eyes.
⁹ The fear of the LORD is pure,
    enduring forever.
The decrees of the LORD are firm,
    and all of them are righteous.
¹⁰ They are more precious than gold,
    than much pure gold;
they are sweeter than honey,
    than honey from the honeycomb.

Psalm 19:1-10

Glory | God's perfect and limitless goodness.
The LORD | Literally *Yahweh*, the name of God.

Statutes, precepts, decrees | Rules/laws.
Righteous | Right in God's eyes; perfectly good.

---

1. According to verse 1, the heavens and the skies are telling us something. What is it?

They tell us about the "glory" of God, which is shown through the work of his hands. Because the heavens and the skies are so beautiful, they point us towards the endless goodness (the glory) of the one who made them.

2. When and where can that message be heard, according to verses 2-4?

It can be heard every day and every night (verse 2), throughout the earth (verse 4).

3. Let's take a look at verse 4. It says, "God has pitched a tent for the sun". What do you think we're being told here about what God is like?

God is spectacularly, unimaginably immense and powerful. He rules over the sun.

But the tent is also a symbol of protection. God not only creates the world and everything in it. He also sustains and nurtures it.

4. From verse 7 onwards, the writer begins talking about "the law of the LORD", the Bible. What do verses 7 and 8 say about God's words, and the effect they will have on us if we listen to them?

- God's words are perfect and trustworthy (verse 7).
- They are right and radiant (verse 8).
- God's words refresh the soul and make us wise (verse 7).
- They give us joy and light – they enable us to see clearly (verse 8).

5. Think of the popular views many people have about God. How does the God we've seen in Genesis 1 and Psalm 19 differ from some of these?

Genesis 1 and Psalm 19 show that God is overwhelmingly creative, kind, generous, and powerful. In other words, the God revealed here is good!

He's a personal, relational God, and not a blind or impersonal "force".

God is a Trinity. This means three divine Persons united in one divine nature. Each of these Persons relate to each other in selfless, joyful love.

He created us out of that overflowing love – not because he needed someone to love, or because he needed us to love him, but so that we could share in his joy.

Because the greatest joy a human being can experience is to know God, the greatest gift God could give us is himself.

(If guests mention the fact that God also acts in judgment, acknowledge the comment and say that we'll be exploring that theme in the next session.)

6. **If you knew Psalm 19 was true, how would it affect the way you feel about God?**

   The kinds of answers you get might include:

   • God is kinder and more loving than we thought
   • God's rules are good rather than designed to spoil our fun
   • We would take God's laws / the Bible more seriously
   • We would read the Bible to find out more about God
   • We would begin to trust that God is good, etc.

7. **(If time) What has been most striking for you during this session?**

   This question helps you move naturally into one-to-one conversations at the end of the session.

SESSION 2
THE TRUSTWORTHY GOD

▷ **Hotel Part 1** (10 min 12 sec)

💬 **What's your current view of God, and how did you reach that viewpoint?** (5 minutes, page 15 of Handbook.)

Note: Avoid commenting as people give their answers. At this stage, don't feel that you need to defend God if you think that what someone says is untrue or unfair.

📖 **We're going to watch the next film now. By way of introduction, let me read you a little bit of Genesis chapter 3.** (Page 16 of Handbook.)

¹ Now the serpent was more crafty than any of the wild animals the LORD God had made. He said to the woman, "Did God really say, 'You must not eat from any tree in the garden'?"

² The woman said to the serpent, "We may eat fruit from the trees in the garden, ³ but God did say, 'You must not eat fruit from the tree that is in the middle of the garden, and you must not touch it, or you will die.'"

⁴ "You will not certainly die," the serpent said to the woman. ⁵ "For God knows that when you eat from it your eyes will be opened, and you will be like God, knowing good and evil."

⁶ *When the woman saw that the fruit of the tree was good for food and pleasing to the eye, and also desirable for gaining wisdom, she took some and ate it. She also gave some to her husband, who was with her, and he ate it.*

Genesis 3:1-6

Crafty | Deceitful.
Garden | The Garden of Eden.

Your eyes will be opened | You will understand new things.

▷ **Hotel Part 2** (14 min 50 sec)

Note: The following talk summary is on page 17 of the Handbook.

• What if the God we don't believe in, or the God we don't trust, isn't actually the God revealed in the Bible?

• Adam and Eve rejected God because they believed a lie about him: they thought they would be happier and more fulfilled without him.

• We too reject God when we believe that making someone else (or something else) our ultimate authority will be better for us.

• God's response to Adam and Eve's rejection is his response to ours. There's judgment: we face death. But he also pursues us in love, offering a rescue from the death we deserve.

• That rescue would involve God himself entering the world, suffering and even experiencing death. He would take our punishment, so that we don't have to.

• Would you trust God if you knew he loved you enough to give up his life for you?

The reason Adam and Eve choose not to trust God is because they believe a lie about him. They think he's holding them back, so they reject him. We're going to explore God's response to our rejection of him as we look at another part of the Bible: Romans chapter 1. (Page 18 of Handbook.)

18 The wrath of God is being revealed from heaven against all the godlessness and wickedness of people, who suppress the truth by their wickedness, 19 since what may be known about God is plain to them, because God has made it plain to them. 20 For since the creation of the world God's invisible qualities – his eternal power and divine nature – have been clearly seen, being understood from what has been made, so that people are without excuse.

21 For although they knew God, they neither glorified him as God nor gave thanks to him, but their thinking became futile and their foolish hearts were darkened. 22 Although they claimed to be wise, they became fools 23 and exchanged the glory of the immortal God for images made to look like a mortal human being and birds and animals and reptiles.

24 Therefore God gave them over in the sinful desires of their hearts to sexual impurity for the degrading of their bodies with one another. 25 They exchanged the truth about God for a lie, and worshipped and served created things rather than the Creator.

Romans 1:18-25

Wrath | God's settled anger against sin.

Divine | Of, from, or like God.
Degrading | Shaming; dishonouring.

---

1. How does verse 25 say people treat God?

- We exchange the truth about God for a lie.
- We worship and serve created things rather than the Creator (in other words, we replace God with things that are not God).
- This means we treat God the same way Adam and Eve did in Genesis chapter 1.

2. What kinds of things do we "worship and serve" rather than God?

The possibilities are almost endless. Often, we worship and serve things which are good in themselves – but are not God: family, money, sex, approval, health, career, and so on.

Some people may challenge the idea that they "worship" things. If so, remind them that when we put anything or anyone in God's place, that's what we worship. That thing has become more desirable to us than he is (see film script on page 94).

3. How are people described in the passage?

- verse 18 – godless, wicked, suppressing truth
- verse 20 – without excuse
- verse 21 – know God but are ungrateful and foolish (in other words, like Adam and Eve, they don't trust God)
- verse 22 – they think they're wise but they're fools (in other words, they're proud)
- verse 24 – sexually immoral

4. We might say, "But what about people who've never heard of God, or people who think he doesn't exist?" How does this passage – and Psalm 19 from the last session – speak to that question?

- Romans 1:20 says that God's "invisible qualities ... have been clearly seen".
- Psalm 19 says that the sky points to God's glory (Psalm 19:1-4).

- These verses in Romans are not saying that God completely reveals himself in creation – he reveals himself perfectly through his Son, Jesus. But there is enough of God's "power" and "nature" all around us that, if someone refuses to seek God, they are clearly "without excuse" (verse 20).
- Is it possible that we've become desensitized to the wonder of the world we live in?

5. Look again at your answer to question 3. How does God respond to this, according to verse 18?

God responds with wrath – his settled anger against sin.

6. Do you feel that's fair of God? Why or why not?

The kinds of answers you get might include:

- Yes, it's fair – because they are "without excuse" (verse 20) and "knew God" (verse 21).
- No, it's not fair – because who is God to decide what is or isn't evil?
- No, it's not fair – because verse 24 says that "God gave them over" to sexual impurity, etc. (Note: This is an issue that will be looked at in Session 7, "The Joyful God".)

This question gives an opportunity to explore God's justice. Comments you might make are:

- How many of us can say that the descriptions in question 3 have never applied to us? If I'm being honest, I don't live up to my own standards of "goodness", let alone God's.
- If rejecting God unleashes all kinds of suffering, evil and injustice in the world, then isn't it loving of God to strongly oppose that?
- Don't good people oppose evil? So why would we expect a good God to just let evil go unpunished? The alternative would be for God to treat evil as if it didn't matter. Do you think that evil doesn't matter?

7. (If time) What has been most striking for you during this session?

This question helps you move naturally into one-to-one conversations at the end of the session.

SESSION 3
THE GENEROUS GOD

▷ **Gold Part 1** (9 min 48 sec)

≋ **What keeps you going in difficult situations?** (5 minutes, page 23 of Handbook.)

📖 **We're going to watch the next film now. By way of introduction, let me read you a little bit of Genesis chapter 12.** (Page 24 of Handbook.)

¹ The LORD had said to Abram, "Go from your country, your people and your father's household to the land I will show you.

² "I will make you into a great nation,
and I will bless you;
I will make your name great,
and you will be a blessing.
³ I will bless those who bless you,
and whoever curses you I will curse;
and all peoples on earth
will be blessed through you."

Genesis 12:1-3

Abram | Later, God changed Abram's name to Abraham.

Bless/blessing/blessed | Generously given good things by God.

(▷) **Gold Part 2** (11 min 49 sec)

Note: The following talk summary is on page 25 of the Handbook.

- We sometimes think of God as being demanding. But he's overwhelmingly generous.

- God promised that through a man called Abraham, "all peoples on earth will be blessed" (Genesis 12:3). In other words, the "garbage" we see in the world would one day be fixed by one of Abraham's descendants.

- God doesn't choose who to bless based on where a person has come from, what they have (or haven't) done, or what they look like.

- As the story of Abraham and Sarah shows, receiving God's blessings doesn't depend on human effort or ability at all.

- By contrast, the "gods" we tend to live for instead are extremely demanding in terms of human effort.

- The promise to Abraham – that all peoples on earth would be blessed – is fulfilled in Jesus Christ.

📖 **We've been thinking about God's unexpected, undeserved generosity. Here's another example, this time from Luke chapter 19.** (Page 26 of Handbook.)

¹ Jesus entered Jericho and was passing through. ² A man was there by the name of Zacchaeus; he was a chief tax collector and was wealthy. ³ He wanted to see who Jesus was, but because he was short he could not see over the crowd. ⁴ So he ran ahead and climbed a sycamore-fig tree to see him, since Jesus was coming that way.

⁵ When Jesus reached the spot, he looked up and said to him, "Zacchaeus, come down immediately. I must stay at your house today." ⁶ So he came down at once and welcomed him gladly.

[7] All the people saw this and began to mutter, "He has gone to be the guest of a sinner."

[8] But Zacchaeus stood up and said to the Lord, "Look, Lord! Here and now I give half of my possessions to the poor, and if I have cheated anybody out of anything, I will pay back four times the amount."

[9] Jesus said to him, "Today salvation has come to this house, because this man, too, is a son of Abraham. [10] For the Son of Man came to seek and to save the lost."

Luke 19:1-10

Jericho | City near the Jordan river.
Sinner | Someone who puts anything or anyone in God's rightful place.
The Lord | Jesus.
Salvation | Being saved from sin.

Son of Abraham | From Abraham's family line (i.e. Jewish).
Son of Man | A title Jesus often used for himself.

---

1. **Zacchaeus was a wealthy tax collector who worked for the Romans. He would have been seen as a parasite, getting rich by working for the enemy. What "god" do you think Zacchaeus was living for (verse 2)?**

   His "god" was money/wealth.

2. **Given Zacchaeus' reputation, how were the crowd expecting Jesus to treat him (verse 7), and what is the big shock of verse 5?**

   The crowd didn't expect Jesus to "stay at [his] house", or even talk to Zacchaeus. They were expecting Jesus to see Zacchaeus as a "sinner" (verse 7) and reject him.

   The shock of verse 5 is that Jesus wants to spend time with Zacchaeus. To have Jesus stay at a person's house would have been seen by the people as a tremendous honour.

3. **What effect does this have on Zacchaeus, according to verse 6? What evidence is there that Zacchaeus no longer worships the same "god" he did before he met Jesus (verse 8)?**

   • Verse 6: He welcomes Jesus gladly. One translation says, "Zacchaeus quickly climbed down and took Jesus to his house in great excitement and joy".

   • Verse 8: The evidence that Zacchaeus is no longer worshipping money is that he's freely able to give it away. He gives away half his possessions to the poor and offers a very generous payback to those he's cheated.

4. **Religion says, "If you're a good person, God will accept you". What's remarkable about what happens here in verses 5-8?**

   It's the other way around. Jesus FIRST offers this man acceptance, and THEN Zacchaeus responds by becoming a generous man, concerned with the needs of the poor.

   We'll see more of this in future sessions. We can't earn God's acceptance by being "moral" or "spiritual" or "a good person". God freely and generously offers us acceptance, if we'll accept it, through the life and death of his Son, Jesus.

5. **In verse 3, Zacchaeus is looking for someone. In verse 10, Jesus ("the Son of Man") says he's looking for someone as well. Who is he looking for and why?**

   Jesus is looking for (seeking) "the lost". This means people who are lost and hopeless without God.

   Jesus is looking for the lost because he wants to save them. We'll see more in the next session about why people need saving and how Jesus saves us.

6. **If you knew that God related to you the way that Jesus related to Zacchaeus, how would you feel?**

The kinds of answers you get might include:

- Amazed – they never thought God would be like that
- Relieved – they expected God to condemn them for not keeping his rules
- Suspicious – this seems too good to be true, so what's the catch?
- Interested – this isn't the kind of god they expected, so they'd like to know more
- Hopeful – they'd love God to treat them in this way

This question gives an opportunity to explore God's generous grace. Comments you might make are:

When a person realizes how "rich" they are in Christ...

- they don't need to use money to gain the acceptance or approval of others, because God himself already accepts and approves of them.

- they don't need to use money to comfort themselves, because they already have the ultimate comfort of knowing God himself.

- they don't need to be ruled by the fear that if they lose their money, they'll lose their security, because they already have complete security in Christ.

7. **(If time) What has been most striking for you during this session?**

This question helps you move naturally into one-to-one conversations at the end of the session.

SESSION 4
THE LIBERATING GOD

▷ **Lawn Part 1** (6 min 30 sec)

💬 **Often we feel our lives would be complete "if only" we had someone or something. What's your "if only"?** (5 minutes, page 31 of Handbook.)

📖 **We're going to watch the next film now. By way of introduction, let me read you a little bit of Exodus chapter 3.** (Page 32 of Handbook.)

⁷ The LORD said, "I have indeed seen the misery of my people in Egypt. I have heard them crying out because of their slave drivers, and I am concerned about their suffering. ⁸ So I have come down to rescue them from the hand of the Egyptians and to bring them up out of that land into a good and spacious land, a land flowing with milk and honey – the home of the Canaanites, Hittites, Amorites, Perizzites, Hivites and Jebusites. ⁹ And now the cry of the Israelites has reached me, and I have seen the way the Egyptians are oppressing them. ¹⁰ So now, go. I am sending you to Pharaoh to bring my people the Israelites out of Egypt."

Exodus 3:7-10

The LORD | Literally *Yahweh*, the name of God.
Canaanites, Hittites, Amorites, Perizzites, Hivites and Jebusites | Groups of people who lived in the area of Canaan.
Oppressing | Persecuting and mistreating.
Pharaoh | King of Egypt.

▷ **Lawn Part 2** (10 min 50 sec)

Note: The following talk summary is on page 33 of the Handbook.

- Jesus said, "Everyone who sins is a slave to sin" (John 8:34). The history of the Israelite slavery in Egypt points towards the way in which we can be freed from our slavery to sin.

- God sent a series of plagues against Egypt because they'd enslaved and abused his people for 400 years. Eventually, God warned Egypt that if they refused to free the Israelites, the firstborn son in every family would die.

- As a reminder that the Israelites had also sinned and deserved judgment, God warned that this plague would affect them too.

- But there was a way out. They would be spared if the blood of a lamb was put on the doorframes. The lamb died in their place.

- This moment in history pointed towards the much greater liberation that Jesus would one day provide on the cross: he would die in our place. That's why Jesus was called "the Lamb of God" (John 1:29).

- When we put our trust in him, we are freed from the penalty our sin deserves. We're also freed from the power sin has over us, because our "if onlys" are transformed.

📖 **In Matthew 11:27-30, Jesus invites people to come to him for freedom and rest.** (Page 34 of Handbook.)

27 [Jesus said,] "All things have been committed to me by my Father. No one knows the Son except the Father, and no one knows the Father except the Son and those to whom the Son chooses to reveal him.

28 "Come to me, all you who are weary and burdened, and I will give you rest. 29 Take my yoke upon you and learn from me, for I am gentle and humble in heart, and you will find rest for your souls. [30] *For my yoke is easy and my burden is light."*

Matthew 11:27-30

Committed | Handed over, entrusted.
Yoke | A wooden crosspiece placed across the neck of two animals and attached to the plough or cart they are to pull.

---

1. What remarkable things does Jesus say in verse 27 about his relationship with God the Father?

- All things have been committed to Jesus by his Father (this means all knowledge).

- No one knows the Son (Jesus) except the Father (this means no one knows the Son fully, except the Father).

- No one knows the Father, except the Son and those "to whom the Son chooses to reveal him".

2. In verse 27, Jesus says that no one can know God the Father except those Jesus reveals him to. Do you feel it's arrogant of Jesus to make that claim? Why or why not?

As with any claim, it's a question of whether a person can back it up. When we read the Gospels, we see the life of Jesus: a person who really demonstrated God's wisdom and God's power.

There is guidance on answering questions about Jesus being the only way to God in the appendix on page 87.

3. **Verse 28 is an invitation to everyone who feels weary and burdened. Given your own experience, and what we've heard in this session, what kinds of burdens do you think Jesus might be talking about?**

The kinds of answers you get might include:

• The burden of our "if onlys": the endless cycle of thinking certain things will make us feel complete. If we get them, we discover that the feeling doesn't last, and so the cycle begins again.

• The burden of trying to make ourselves "good enough" for God or other people (through religious practices, people-pleasing, etc)

• Our slavery to sin makes us feel weary and burdened: we keep doing it even though we don't want to. Jesus says in John 8:34 that "everyone who sins is a slave to sin".

(If people aren't sure they are slaves to sin, ask them: "All of us instinctively know we ought to treat others in a way we'd want to be treated ourselves. But can we honestly say we always live like that? Without any unkindness or impatience or prejudice?")

4. **Jesus said he came to give his life "as a ransom for many" (Mark 10:45). What does a "ransom" have to do with Jesus' death?**

A ransom is a price paid to set someone free from slavery or captivity. Jesus is saying that he died to set us free from our slavery to sin.

5. **In verse 29 Jesus says, "Take my yoke upon you". What would you say to someone who said, "I'm not becoming anyone's slave!" What kind of master is Jesus, according to verses 28-30?**

Verses 28-30 make it clear what kind of a master Jesus is:

• He is welcoming (he invites people to come to him, verse 28).
• He gives rest (verse 28).

- He teaches (verse 29).
- He is gentle (verse 29).
- He is humble in heart (verse 29).
- In him, people find rest for their souls (verse 29).
- His yoke is easy (verse 30).
- His burden is light (verse 30).

6. What would it feel like to serve a master like this – one who died to set you free?

This question will help people reflect on their response to Jesus.

7. (If time) What has been most striking for you during this session?

This question helps you move naturally into one-to-one conversations at the end of the session.

SESSION 5
THE FULFILLING GOD

▷ **Geisha Part 1** (11 min 59 sec)

☰ **What are you hoping will bring you fulfilment in life?**
(5 minutes, page 39 of Handbook.)

📖 **We're going to watch the next film now. By way of introduction, let me read you a little bit of John chapter 4.** (Page 40 of Handbook.)

⁶ Jesus, tired as he was from the journey, sat down by the well. It was about noon.

⁷ When a Samaritan woman came to draw water, Jesus said to her, "Will you give me a drink?" ⁸ (His disciples had gone into the town to buy food.)

⁹ The Samaritan woman said to him, "You are a Jew and I am a Samaritan woman. How can you ask me for a drink?" (For Jews do not associate with Samaritans.)

¹⁰ Jesus answered her, "If you knew the gift of God and who it is that asks you for a drink, you would have asked him and he would have given you living water."

¹¹ "Sir," the woman said, "you have nothing to draw with and the well is deep. Where can you get this living water? ¹² Are you greater than our father Jacob, who gave us the well and drank from it himself, as did also his sons and his livestock?"

*[13] Jesus answered, "Everyone who drinks this water will be thirsty again,
[14] but whoever drinks the water I give them will never thirst. Indeed, the
water I give them will become in them a spring of water welling up to
eternal life."*

John 4:6-14

Samaritan | From Samaria. Jews and
Samaritans hated each other.
Jacob | Abraham's grandson.

Eternal life | Perfect, sinless life that
lasts forever in the joyful presence of
God.

(▷) **Geisha Part 2** (13 min 12 sec)

Note: The following talk summary is on page 41 of the Handbook.

- We're richer than we've ever been – we have more leisure time, more freedom and more opportunity – yet many of us feel less fulfilled than ever.
  Why?

- Many of us seek fulfilment anywhere but in the place we were designed to
  find it: in God himself.

- Except perhaps for a short time, other sources of fulfilment don't satisfy.
  They weren't intended to. "All our dreams come false."

- In the Old Testament, God identifies himself as "the spring of living water",
  the one who satisfies our deepest thirst for fulfilment.

- In the New Testament, Jesus identifies himself in the same way: "Whoever
  drinks the water I give them will never thirst. Indeed, the water I give them
  will become in them a spring of water welling up to eternal life" (John 4:14).

📖 **Jesus told a story about two sons, and the places where each son looked for fulfilment. The younger son seeks fulfilment by demanding his inheritance while his father is still alive, and spending it on prostitutes and wild living. You can see what happens next in Luke 15.** (Page 42 of Handbook.)

[14] *"After he had spent everything, there was a severe famine in that whole country, and he began to be in need. [15] So he went and hired himself out to a citizen of that country, who sent him to his fields to feed pigs. [16] He longed to fill his stomach with the pods that the pigs were eating, but no one gave him anything.*

[17] *"When he came to his senses, he said, 'How many of my father's hired servants have food to spare, and here I am starving to death! [18] I will set out and go back to my father and say to him: Father, I have sinned against heaven and against you. [19] I am no longer worthy to be called your son; make me like one of your hired servants.' [20] So he got up and went to his father.*

"But while he was still a long way off, his father saw him and was filled with compassion for him; he ran to his son, threw his arms round him and kissed him.

[21] *"The son said to him, 'Father, I have sinned against heaven and against you. I am no longer worthy to be called your son.'*

[22] *"But the father said to his servants, 'Quick! Bring the best robe and put it on him. Put a ring on his finger and sandals on his feet. [23] Bring the fattened calf and kill it. Let's have a feast and celebrate. [24] For this son of mine was dead and is alive again; he was lost and is found.' So they began to celebrate.*

[25] *"Meanwhile, the older son was in the field. When he came near the house, he heard music and dancing. [26] So he called one of the servants and asked him what was going on. [27] 'Your brother has come,' he replied, 'and your father has killed the fattened calf because he has him back safe and sound.'*

[28] *"The older brother became angry and refused to go in. So his father went out and pleaded with him. [29] But he answered his father, 'Look! All these years*

I've been slaving for you and never disobeyed your orders. Yet you never gave me even a young goat so I could celebrate with my friends. ³⁰ But when this son of yours who has squandered your property with prostitutes comes home, you kill the fattened calf for him!'

³¹ "'My son,' the father said, 'you are always with me, and everything I have is yours. ³² But we had to celebrate and be glad, because this brother of yours was dead and is alive again; he was lost and is found.'"

Luke 15:14-32

Pods | Seed pods from the carob tree, used to feed animals.
Sinned | Done wrong; rebelled against.

Fattened calf | The best calf, set aside for a special celebration.
Squandered | Wasted.

---

1. **If you were in the younger brother's position in verses 17-19, what kind of response would you be expecting from your father? What's staggering about the father's response in verse 20?**

   • The younger brother might expect anger, punishment, and possibly rejection. (The younger brother demanded the inheritance from his father while his father was still alive. It's as if he'd said to his father, "I wish you were dead".)

   • It's surprising that the father shows extraordinary compassion, affection and acceptance to his younger son. He runs to him, embraces him and kisses him! The father doesn't bring up the past – he is simply overwhelmed with joy that his son has returned to him.

2. **The father forgives his son. But he does much more than that. Given that the father in the story represents God, how else do we see God's lavish goodness reflected in verses 22-25?**

God's goodness doesn't just end with forgiveness. The father throws a huge party for his younger son! He puts the best clothes on him (verse 22), prepares the best food for him (verse 23), tells the band to start playing (verse 25), and gets the dancing started (verse 25).

This is what life is like with God. He doesn't forgive people in order to make them miserable – he wants us to be happy and fulfilled in him.

3. **The older brother thinks of himself as a very good person who always obeys his father (verse 29). What kind of person does that turn him into? (See verses 28-30.)**

Angry, stubborn, entitled, bitter and resentful. The older brother feels he's done lots of good things for his father – so now his father owes him.

This is a huge danger for people who see themselves as very moral or very religious – rather than seeing that they owe everything to God, they can start to feel that God owes *them*.

4. **The father tells the older brother in verse 31, "You are always with me, and everything I have is yours". Although the older brother already knows this, he's still angry (verses 28-30). Clearly his father's love isn't enough for him. If he's not finding fulfilment in his father's love, where *is* he looking for it?**

The older brother looks for fulfilment in what he's done and what he believes he deserves.

His sense of fulfilment doesn't come from knowing and loving his father. It comes from feeling morally superior to others (e.g. his younger brother). That's why he resents his father's goodness towards his brother.

5. **At the beginning of the story, where does the younger brother look for fulfilment? By the end of the story, where does he find it?**

At the beginning, the younger brother looks for fulfilment in money, prostitutes and wild living.

At the end, he finds fulfilment in restored relationship with his father, who forgives him, welcomes him back, and throws a party to celebrate.

6. **Both brothers needed the father's forgiveness: one for his immorality and one for his "morality". What do we learn from the younger brother about how to approach God? And what do we learn from the older brother about how *not* to approach God?**

The younger brother comes back to his father humbly, knowing he deserves nothing. Like the younger brother, whatever we've done wrong, we ought to "go back" to the father (verse 18), acknowledge what we've done (verses 18-19), and throw ourselves on his mercy (verse 21).

The older brother is a warning, particularly to people who think of themselves as very good, moral or religious people, that we should beware of coming to God with a sense of entitlement. God doesn't owe us anything; we owe *him* everything.

7. **(If time) What has been most striking for you during this session?**

This question helps you move naturally into one-to-one conversations at the end of the session.

SESSION 6
THE LIFE-GIVING GOD

▷ **Celebrity Part 1** (6 min 46 sec)

💬 **What, if you lost it, would make you feel that life wasn't worth living?** (5 minutes, page 47 of Handbook.)

📖 **We're going to watch the next film now. By way of introduction, let me read you a little bit of 1 Corinthians chapter 15.** (Page 48 of Handbook.)

³ What I received I passed on to you as of first importance: that Christ died for our sins according to the Scriptures, ⁴ that he was buried, that he was raised on the third day according to the Scriptures, ⁵ and that he appeared to Cephas, and then to the Twelve. ⁶ After that, he appeared to more than five hundred of the brothers and sisters at the same time, most of whom are still living, though some have fallen asleep. ⁷ Then he appeared to James, then to all the apostles, ⁸ and last of all he appeared to me also.

1 Corinthians 15:3-8

Christ | Jesus.
Sins | Putting anything or anyone in God's rightful place.
Scriptures | The Old Testament part of the Bible.
Raised | Brought from death to life.
Cephas | Another name for Peter.
The Twelve | Jesus' twelve closest followers, often called the disciples.

Brothers and sisters | Fellow Christians.
Fallen asleep | Died.
James | One of the twelve disciples.
Apostles | "Apostle" means "one sent as a messenger". The apostles were sent by Jesus to tell the world about him.

(▷) **Celebrity Part 2** (14 min 10 sec)

Note: The following talk summary is on page 49 of the Handbook.

• If we trust in anything other than God for our ultimate security, we will "die a million deaths" before we actually die.

• When we live for power, approval, comfort or control, then when we don't get those things, we feel as if life isn't worth living.

• These "gods" we live for promise us life, but they can't deliver us from death.

• Jesus demonstrated that he *can* deliver us from death. He proved that by actually overcoming death himself.

• Jesus' resurrection delivers us, not just from a literal death, but also from the "million deaths" we will suffer before we die if we've put our trust in power, approval, comfort or control.

• A person can only stop trusting these idols if their desire for something else is greater. We need to see Jesus Christ as more desirable to us than anything else.

📖 **One of Jesus' followers, Paul, once spoke to the people of Athens about hope in the face of death. This is Acts chapter 17.** (Page 50 of Handbook.)

[22] *"People of Athens! I see that in every way you are very religious.* [23] *For as I walked around and looked carefully at your objects of worship, I even found an altar with this inscription: 'To an unknown god'. So you are ignorant of the very thing you worship – and this is what I am going to proclaim to you.*

[24] *"The God who made the world and everything in it is the Lord of heaven and earth and does not live in temples built by human hands.* [25] *And he is not served by human hands, as if he needed anything. Rather, he himself gives everyone life and breath and everything else.* [26] *From one man he made all the nations, that they should inhabit the whole earth; and he marked out their appointed times in history and the boundaries of their lands.* [27] *God did this so that they would seek him and perhaps reach out for him and find him, though he is not far from any one of us.* [28] *'For in him we live and move and have our being.' As some of your own poets have said, 'We are his offspring.'*

[29] *"Therefore since we are God's offspring, we should not think that the divine being is like gold or silver or stone – an image made by human design and skill.* [30] *In the past God overlooked such ignorance, but now he commands all people everywhere to repent.* [31] *For he has set a day when he will judge the world with justice by the man he has appointed. He has given proof of this to everyone by raising him from the dead."*

Acts 17:22-31

Religious | Devoted to a god or gods.
Proclaim | Announce/tell.
Offspring | Children and descendants.

The divine being | God
Repent | To turn away from sin and turn back to God.

---

1. **In verse 22 Paul says, "I see that in every way you are very religious". From your own experience, do you think "non-religious" or "anti-religious" people can be religious?**

   If your group struggle to answer this, explain that being "religious" can mean being devoted to something. Everyone devotes their life to something or someone. It could be family or fame, approval or comfort, sex or sport, or a hundred other things. We might even say, "Sport is my religion" or "I weigh myself religiously every day".

2. **Paul then compares the real God with the false gods that people worship instead. Who is the real "Lord of heaven and earth", according to the first bit of verse 24? How is this God different to their idols, according to the end of verse 24?**

   He's "the God who made the world and everything in it".

   God doesn't live in temples built by human hands.

3. **What's the other difference between God and idols, according to verse 25?**

   Unlike our "idols", God doesn't need us to serve him. It's not as if he lacks anything. "He himself gives everyone life and breath and everything else", which means *we* are the ones who need *him*.

4. **From what you've heard in this session, how do you think the following idols "need" to be served?**

   • **physical beauty**
   • **approval of others**
   • **money**

   • If our idol is physical beauty, then we *must* keep measuring up to a certain standard, and when we fail, we feel devastated.

- If our idol is the approval of others, then we *must* keep getting it, otherwise we feel worthless.

- If our idol is money, then we *must* keep earning "enough", otherwise we feel our lives are a failure and we become miserable.

Idols make terrible, unattainable demands on us.

By contrast, God's love for a person doesn't depend on us "measuring up" to certain demands. God's Son has already "measured up" for us, on our behalf, if we put our trust in him.

5. The resurrection shows that, in Christ, we can have life after death. Look again at verse 31. What else does the resurrection show?

- God has set a day when he will judge the world.
- He will judge the world with justice (so his judgment will be right and good).
- God has appointed (chosen) the man who will be the judge.
- He proved this by raising that man from the dead.
- This means the man chosen by God to be Judge of the whole world is Jesus, who was raised from the dead by his Father, God.

Note: If people ask how we can know the resurrection really happened, suggest talking about it after the session (see pages 85 and 87 for help in answering this question).

6. If we've come to realize that we've been serving idols rather than "the God who made the world and everything in it" (verse 24), what must we do, according to verse 30? What would it take for you to do this?

We must repent. This means we must turn back to God, and away from our idols.

Repentance isn't something you do once and then forget about. It's something we have to keep doing. All of us struggle with idols. As one person put it, our hearts are "factories of idols".

So we must keep turning back to God, remembering with joy that this is the God who, in Jesus, died so that we could live.

At this point, you might want to say, "If you haven't turned back to God, let me encourage you to do that. Have a word with me at the end of this session if that's something you want to do or think about." (For more guidance on this, see question 6 in session 7, and pages 78-80 in this Leader's Handbook.)

7. (If time) What has been most striking for you during this session?

This question helps you move naturally into one-to-one conversations at the end of the session.

SESSION 7
THE JOYFUL GOD

▷ **Space Part 1** (9 min 07 sec)

💬 **Now that we've reached the end of *Life Explored*, think again about the question we asked at the very beginning, and see if your answer is any different: What's the best gift God could give you?** (5 minutes, page 55 of Handbook.)

Note: This question will help people reflect on whether their view of God has changed during *Life Explored*. There's no need to comment on people's answers at this point, though you may like to do so one to one after the end of the session.

📖 **We're going to watch the next film now. By way of introduction, let me read you a little bit of Revelation chapter 21.** (Page 56 of Handbook.)

¹ Then I saw "a new heaven and a new earth," for the first heaven and the first earth had passed away, and there was no longer any sea. ² I saw the Holy City, the new Jerusalem, coming down out of heaven from God, prepared as a bride beautifully dressed for her husband. ³ And I heard a loud voice from the throne saying, "Look! God's dwelling-place is now among the people, and he will dwell with them. They will be his people, and God himself will be with them and be their God. ⁴ 'He will wipe every tear from their eyes. There will be no more death' or mourning or crying or pain, for the old order of things has passed away."

*⁵ He who was seated on the throne said, "I am making everything new!"
Then he said, "Write this down, for these words are trustworthy and true."*

*⁶ He said to me: "It is done. I am the Alpha and the Omega, the Beginning
and the End. To the thirsty I will give water without cost from the spring of
the water of life. ⁷ Those who are victorious will inherit all this, and I will be
their God and they will be my children."*

Revelation 21:1-7

Holy City | Jerusalem.
Dwell | Live.
The old order of things | How things
used to be.

Alpha and Omega | The first and last
letters in the Greek alphabet.

▷ **Space Part 2** (14 min 59 sec)

Note: The following talk summary is on page 57 of the Handbook.

- There is, inside each one of us, a longing for relationship, and a longing for home.

- And yet many of us feel that our earthly relationships and our earthly homes never fully satisfy – not even the best ones.

- That's because we were made for another world. The Bible calls it "a new heaven and a new earth" (Revelation 21:1) – a world, real and physical, where we experience both the relationship and the home we've longed for all our lives.

- This new world is described as being like a joyful wedding between Jesus Christ (the bridegroom) and his people (the bride).

- Jesus speaks of those who are shut out from the new heaven and new earth because of their idolatry. As with any wedding, not everyone will be there.

- If you're not living for Christ, which god are you living for instead? Does it give you lasting freedom, fulfilment or peace? Does it have an answer to death? Has it laid down its life for you? Is your god as good as this God has shown himself to be?

In our final discussion, we're going to look at Matthew 22, where Jesus tells a story about a wedding. (Page 58 of Handbook.)

² "The kingdom of heaven is like a king who prepared a wedding banquet for his son. ³ He sent his servants to those who had been invited to the banquet to tell them to come, but they refused to come.

⁴ "Then he sent some more servants and said, 'Tell those who have been invited that I have prepared my dinner: my oxen and fattened cattle have been slaughtered, and everything is ready. Come to the wedding banquet.'

⁵ "But they paid no attention and went off – one to his field, another to his business. ⁶ The rest seized his servants, ill-treated them and killed them. ⁷ The king was enraged. He sent his army and destroyed those murderers and burned their city.

⁸ "Then he said to his servants, 'The wedding banquet is ready, but those I invited did not deserve to come. ⁹ So go to the street corners and invite to the banquet anyone you find.' ¹⁰ So the servants went out into the streets and gathered all the people they could find, the bad as well as the good, and the wedding hall was filled with guests.

¹¹ "But when the king came in to see the guests, he noticed a man there who was not wearing wedding clothes. ¹² He asked, 'How did you get in here without wedding clothes, friend?' The man was speechless.

¹³ "Then the king told the attendants, 'Tie him hand and foot, and throw him outside, into the darkness, where there will be weeping and gnashing of teeth.'

¹⁴ "For many are invited, but few are chosen."

Matthew 22:2-14

Kingdom of heaven | The place where God's people live joyfully under God's rule.
Wedding clothes | In those days it was the custom to give wedding guests particular clothes to wear to the banquet.
Gnashing | Grinding.

1. **The king invites guests to his son's wedding banquet three times. He is persistent, patient and generous. What are the different ways in which the invited guests respond in verses 3, 5 and 6?**

   - Verse 3: They refuse to come.
   - Verse 5: They ignore the invitation because they value their possessions and career more.
   - Verse 6: Some seize the king's servants, mistreat them and kill them.

2. **The king in Jesus' story represents God. In verses 7-10, the king responds to this treason in two ways. What are they?**

   - Verse 7: Anger. He destroys the murderers and their city.
   - Verses 8-10: Undeserved generosity and kindness. He throws open his invitation to everyone, "the bad as well as the good" (verse 10).

3. **In verse 13, a man is thrown out of the wedding banquet. Why?**

   The man was not wearing wedding clothes. (In those days it was the custom to give wedding guests particular clothes to wear to the banquet.)

4. **Isaiah 61:10 says:**
   "I delight greatly in the LORD;
   my soul rejoices in my God.
   For he has clothed me with garments of salvation
   and arrayed me in a robe of his righteousness."

   What do you think the "wedding clothes" might represent in Jesus' story, and where do they come from?

The wedding clothes represent salvation and righteousness. (Righteousness is a word that means perfect goodness.)

They come from God ("*he* has clothed me").

We can't clothe ourselves for this particular wedding. That means we can't rely on our own attempts at goodness to gain access. Only God can provide the righteousness we need.

5. **Given what we've learned about God's character during *Life Explored*, why do you think God offers people salvation, and how has he made that possible?**

God is good, generous and life-giving. He wants us to enjoy the best gift he can give us – himself.

He has made this possible through the life, death and resurrection of Jesus. This is explained in 2 Corinthians 5:21, which says, "God made him who had no sin to be sin for us, so that in him we might become the righteousness of God".

If we are "in Christ", then we are "clothed" with his righteousness. When we put our trust in Christ, we have his perfect goodness credited to us.

How is this possible? Christ "put on" human sin, when he died on the cross. He willingly took the punishment we deserve. As a result, we can now "put on" Christ's righteousness, by simply trusting in him.

Note: If people say salvation is possible because of their own good deeds, ask them to look again at Matthew 22:10, which says that the king invited "the bad as well as the good". People are invited not on the basis of their good deeds, but on the basis of Jesus' good deeds on their behalf.

6. **If you had to cast yourself in this story, which one of these four characters would you be?**

   Do you see other things as more valuable to you than being at the Son's banquet (verse 5)?

   Would you consider yourself to be hostile to the invitation (verse 6)?

   Do you feel you're already acceptable to God, without needing the "wedding clothes" he provides (verse 11)?

   Or would you accept the invitation to the Son's wedding banquet?

   This question helps you get a sense of how best to pick up one-to-one conversations when the session ends.

7. **(If time) What has been most striking for you during this session?**

   This question helps you move naturally into one-to-one conversations at the end of the session. Before you officially end the session, thank everyone for making time for *Life Explored*! Invite them to come to church with you next Sunday as your guest.

Guidance for one-to-one conversations after the last session

For those who feel that other things are more valuable to them, you might ask, "What do you think it would take for you to feel that Jesus is more valuable?"

For those who want to reject the invitation, you might start the conversation by asking, "What is it about Jesus you're unsure of?"

For those who feel they're "good enough" as they are, you might look at what Jesus says later in Matthew 22:36-39. Ask, "How do you think we're doing in terms of keeping the first and most important command?"

For those who want to accept the invitation. Rejoice! Explain that Jesus calls us to repent and believe in him (Mark 1:15). In other words, we turn away from our love and worship of things that are not God, and turn back towards the God who loves us and gave his Son so we could enjoy him forever. Ask them what they think that might look like for them. Arrange to meet again as soon as possible. (See page 20 for more on how to help someone who wants to become a Christian.)

For everyone. Invite them to come to church with you as your guest next Sunday. Think about how you can stay in touch. Keep praying.

Other suggestions:

• Give your guests Bibles and books to take away with them. This is a great way to help people pick up from where *Life Explored* ends.

Some recommended titles:

One Life by Rico Tice and Barry Cooper. A walk through Mark's Gospel, exploring who Jesus is, why he came, and what it means to follow him.

Can I Really Trust The Bible? by Barry Cooper. Explores the big questions people have about the Bible, and encourages the reader to "taste and see" for themselves.

If You Could Ask God One Question by Paul Williams and Barry Cooper. A look at ten frequently asked questions, each one answered from the lips of Jesus.

Explore Bible-reading notes by The Good Book Company. A good starting point would be *Explore: Time with God* – 28 Bible readings to get people started in a regular time with God. Available as a printed booklet or via the free Explore App.

• Invite people to any future courses you're running.

Christianity Explored is designed for both Christians and non-Christians. It explores a single book of the Bible (Mark's Gospel) in more depth.

Discipleship Explored is for Christians, even those who've only just started following Jesus. It also explores a single book of the Bible (Paul's letter to the Philippians) in more depth.

• For short video answers to tough questions, direct people to **www.christianity.explo.red**

APPENDICES

QUESTIONS ABOUT
CHRISTIAN BELIEF

How do you know that God exists?

- Many philosophical and scientific arguments have been used over the years to show that believing in God is rational and sensible. But ultimately, even the best of these lead only to general belief in a God, not specifically to the God of the Bible. It is usually more helpful to talk about Jesus and his claim to be God.

- We can know God exists because he became a man: Jesus Christ. This is the core of Jesus' answer to Philip's question in John 14:8-9. It's worth looking this up and reading it together if the question arises.

- Jesus was a real person who lived in Palestine 2000 years ago – the historical evidence for this stacks up (see next question).

- Jesus claimed to be God (e.g. John 5:18; 20:28-29). If those claims are borne out by Jesus' life, then that would be the strongest possible proof that God does indeed exist.

Why should we believe what the Bible says?

- Again, our answer to this question will depend on our view of Jesus. What's clear from the Gospels is that Jesus trusted the Bible implicitly. So, if we believe Jesus himself is trustworthy, it follows that the Bible is trustworthy.

- Try not to get bogged down in defending passages from all over the Bible. Instead, for the sake of clarity, focus on the reliability of the Gospels. If what they contain about Jesus is reliable, then his words about the trustworthiness of Scripture as a whole come into play.

- The Gospels were written within living memory of the public events they record. Yet none of the first readers were able to disprove the claims made about Jesus' life, death and resurrection.

- Textual criticism shows that the text of these documents has come down to us intact from the era in which they were written.

- The New Testament writers kept insisting on the truth of the history they'd recorded, even though they knew it would likely lead to persecution, torture and death. They were so convinced they had seen and touched and interacted with Jesus, after he had been publicly executed and buried, that they were prepared to die rather than lie about what they'd witnessed.

- The Gospels are very uncomplimentary about the disciples who assisted in writing them. For example, Peter helped Mark write his Gospel – and yet Peter is shown to be a coward (Mark 14:66-72). Given that Peter was a leader in the early church, why would he include something like this? Unless, of course, it was just the inconvenient truth.

- The Gospel accounts are too detailed to be legends. They're packed full of tiny details that apparently serve no purpose, unless explained simply as eyewitness details. Modern novels sometimes have this level of detail, but they didn't exist until about 300 years ago; it's unprecedented in an ancient document. The author C.S. Lewis (once Professor of English Literature at both Oxford and Cambridge) said, "I have been reading poems, romances, vision literature, legends and myths all my life. I know what they are like. I know none of them are like this."

- For more detail on these and other Bible-related questions, Barry Cooper's *Can I Really Trust The Bible?* is a brief, accessible read aimed at non-Christians as well as Christians.

Isn't the Bible out of date socially, culturally and sexually?

- If the Bible is a product of its time and place, aren't we also products of our time and place? For example, social and sexual ethics that seem self-evidently true to a 21st-century person living in London aren't self-evidently true to most people currently living in Nairobi – or those who were living in London 50 years ago. How can we be sure that we, in our own particular time and place, know best?

- If we feel discomfort at some of the Bible's teaching, is it really because the Bible is a product of its time, or because we are?

- If the Bible really were God's word, wouldn't it be highly suspicious if it always happened to agree with us on our particular views, in our particular moment of history?

Don't all good people go to heaven?

- What is "good"? How good is "good enough"?

- Some of us are better than others, but no one meets God's standards (see Romans 3:23).

- We are not good, because our hearts are "sin factories" (Mark 7:21-22).

- People who think they're "good enough" for heaven don't realize that they've broken what Jesus calls the first and most important of all God's commands: "Love the Lord your God with all your heart and with all your soul and with all your mind and with all your strength" (Mark 12:28-30). Rather than loving God, we love other things more (see the story of the rich man meeting Jesus in Mark 10:17-22). We may be "good" relative to others, but we can't be good enough for heaven if we break God's most important command.

- The opposite is, in fact, true. "Good" people go to hell; bad people go to heaven. Those who think they are good, and rely on that, will be lost. Only those who know they are lost are able to receive forgiveness and eternal life from Christ.

Why would a good God send people to hell?

- God is utterly holy and good. His character is what decides right and wrong in the universe.

- God must judge everyone. He would not be a just God if he ignored wrongdoing or evil. He will judge fairly and well.

- We know that punishments ought to fit the crime. Someone who murders deserves a worse punishment than someone who runs a red light. Is it possible that the reason we think hell is unfair is because we don't realize how serious our sin is?

- Jesus is the most loving person who ever lived, but it is he who teaches most about the reality of hell. He does so because he knows it is real, and doesn't want us to suffer the inevitable consequences of our rebellion against God.

- When Jesus died on the cross, he was dying in our place. For those who turn to him, Jesus took the punishment we deserve, so we can know God and enjoy him forever. Jesus went through hell, so we don't have to.

- If we understood how holy God is, we would be asking the opposite question: how can God allow anyone into heaven?

If God forgives everything, does that mean I can do what I like?

- God offers us forgiveness so that we can know and enjoy him. Why would we want to "do what we like" if doing so keeps us from enjoying him to the full, and puts us in danger of judgment?

How can we be sure that there is life after death?

- The Bible teaches that everyone will be resurrected after death in order to face judgment (Hebrews 9:27). For those who know and love Christ, there is nothing to fear, because the One appointed as Judge (Acts 17:31) is also the One who gave his life for them.

- Who do you trust for accurate information about life beyond the grave? The person who has been there and come back. If Jesus has been raised from the dead, then those who trust in him will also be delivered from death. (See John 11:25.)

What about other religions?

- Sincerity is not truth. People can be sincerely wrong.

- If the different religions contradict each other (which they do at several major points), they cannot all be right.

- The question really is: has God revealed himself, and if so, how? Jesus claimed to be the unique revelation of God. He claimed to be God in the flesh. Are his claims valid? If Jesus is God, then logically, other religions must be wrong.

- Jesus claims he is the only way (John 14:6).

- Religions can do many good things: provide comfort, help, social bonding, etc. But all of them – apart from Christianity – teach that we must DO something in order to "earn" our place in heaven.

- By contrast, Jesus claims that we can never "earn" our way to heaven by doing good things. He claims that the only way we can know and enjoy God forever is if we trust in what HE (Jesus) has done on our behalf, not in what WE have done.

What about those who have never heard about Jesus?

- We can trust God to be just; he will judge people according to their response to what they know.

- Everyone has received some revelation, even if only from the created world (see Romans 1:18-19).

- Those who have had more revealed to them will be held more responsible (Matthew 11:20-24).

- You have heard, so you must do something about it – and leave the others to God, who will treat them fairly.

Isn't faith just a psychological crutch?

- It is true that faith in Christ provides an enormous psychological crutch! It gives hope, meaning and joy, even in the face of suffering and death. It is one of life's greatest joys to know for certain that you are perfectly known and yet perfectly loved by the Creator of the universe.

- But that doesn't mean Christian faith is "wishful thinking", some sort of imaginary story created to make us feel better in the face of life's hardships.

- On the contrary, Christian faith is founded on historical events: the life, death and resurrection of Jesus. The truth of these events – and therefore the truth of Christianity – doesn't depend on whether or not we "need" them to be true.

Why would I give up my freedom to follow Christ, or anyone else?

- Don't we know from our own experience that to enjoy certain freedoms, we must give up others? The skier who wants to enjoy the freedom of the slopes must give up the "freedom" to ignore the warning signs at the cliff edge. The person who wants to enjoy the freedom and security that comes from a good marriage must give up certain freedoms they may have had as a single person.

- In the same way, Jesus said that true freedom only comes from following him. This is because "everyone who sins is a slave to sin" (John 8:34), and Christ is the only one who can release people from that slavery: "If you hold to my teaching … you will know the truth, and the truth will set you free" (John 8:31-32).

Why does God allow suffering?

- Much suffering is a direct result of our own sinfulness (e.g. that caused by drunkenness, greed, lust, etc.).

- But some is not (see John 9:1-3).

- All suffering results from the fallen nature of our world (see Romans 8:18-25).

- God uses suffering to discipline and strengthen his children (see Hebrews 12:7-11; Romans 5:3-5).

- God also uses suffering to wake people up so that they understand that there is a judgment coming to our pain-filled world (Luke 13:1-5).

- Unlike many other "gods", the God of the Bible knows intimately what it is like to suffer. God the Son suffered loneliness, grief, temptation, alienation from loved ones, mockery, isolation, bereavement, hunger, thirst, homelessness, mental anguish and the worst physical agonies humans have been able to invent. As a result, he relates to and sympathizes with our deepest pain (Hebrews 4:15). He is not distant from it, or disinterested in it.

- But the God of the Bible does more than show mere sympathy; he has done something decisive to end all human suffering. Jesus suffered and died so that those who know and love him can one day enjoy a new creation, where there will be no suffering or pain of any kind.

- Though we don't know all the reasons why God allows suffering in every case, it seems reasonable to assume that our "not knowing" doesn't necessarily mean suffering must be pointless. At the time Jesus suffered and died, the disciples would have felt that his death was a horrible evil, a pointless tragedy. And yet, if the biblical claim is true, his suffering and death was the means by which countless millions of lives have been saved.

- "With time and perspective most of us can see good reasons for at least some of the tragedy and pain that occurs in life. Why couldn't it be possible that, from God's vantage point, there are good reasons for all of them?" – Tim Keller

Hasn't science disproved Christianity?

- Start by asking what they mean by the question. They may have some specific point which needs addressing – and that will require some research. During the session, it's best to avoid having technical discussions about evolution, carbon dating, etc. as you're likely to run over time, or leave other members of the group bored or left out.

- Most people mean, "Hasn't the theory of (macro)evolution replaced the idea of creation, and so disproved Christianity?" People usually are not talking about archaeology which, incidentally, backs up the Bible at almost every point.

- Ask what conclusions they are drawing from evolution. Even if they believe it gives an account of how life on earth came to be so varied, it doesn't answer the question of how life came to be in the first place. How did something come from nothing – literally nothing, not even empty space. It also doesn't answer the question of WHY things exist: what is the purpose of life? What should we live FOR?

- Steer the conversation towards talking about God's existence (see above) and towards Jesus. If Jesus is God, it puts the creation/evolution debate in a completely different perspective.

If Jesus is God's Son, how can he be God too?

- Jesus lets himself be described as the "Son of God" – a term which can mean that he is the King of God's people, but can also be a claim that he is much more.

- Jesus acts in the New Testament in the way that God does in the Old Testament. He speaks as God speaks, and does things that only God can do (raises the dead, forgives sins, controls nature, etc.). His words and actions show that he is making a claim to be God.

- Christians do not believe that there are many gods, and that Jesus is just one of them. The Bible teaches that God is a "tri-unity" or "Trinity": one God in three "Persons". The three Persons are Father, Son and Spirit, all of whom are fully God. For one example of this biblical teaching, see the description of Jesus' baptism in Mark 1:10-11, where God's tri-unity is clearly seen.

- This is complex and hard to grasp fully – but wouldn't it be strange if the nature of God himself were an easy thing for finite humans to understand?

Why does God hate sex?
- It would be odd if the Creator of sex hated it! He created sex to be beautiful, enjoyable and extremely powerful.

- Isn't it likely that our Creator knows best what leads to our joy and health? He designed sex to be enjoyed by a husband and wife within the mutual protection of marriage (see Jesus' words in Matthew 19:4-5). Sex joins people together in a way that is more than physical.

- Marriage is a temporary institution which anticipates and reflects a far greater marriage: the marriage of God and his people, which God's people will enjoy in the new creation. This is why Jesus is described as the bridegroom and his people are portrayed as his bride (Revelation 19:7-9).

- But those who, for whatever reason, remain single all their lives will not miss out on anything if their hope is in Christ. Not even the very best earthly marriage will come close to the experience of being fully known and loved in the new creation (Revelation 19:7-9).

Christians are hypocrites – so how can Christianity be true?
- The failure of many Christians to live according to their stated beliefs does not invalidate Jesus' claims to be God.

- The Bible says that Jesus alone is perfect, and it is honest about the failures and weakness of his followers.

- Jesus taught that there will always be false teachers and fakes (Mark 13:21-22) who pretend they are Christians but who are not. This is true today.

- Everyone is a hypocrite to some extent. How many of us fully and perfectly "practise what we preach"? But Jesus calls those who follow him to grow more like him.

Note: For answers to these and other questions, see *If You Could Ask God One Question* by Paul Williams and Barry Cooper. It's ideal for leaders and for group members. More technical but still very readable is *The Reason for God* by Tim Keller.

FILM
SCRIPTS

Each session of *Life Explored* includes two films, with each complementing the other. For more on this, see page 10.

The first films are essentially wordless, but the scripts for the second films are given below. They're included here for easy reference during a session, and also to help you prepare beforehand.

Session 1: Overture

Human beings are the glory and the garbage of the universe. That was something the French scientist Blaise Pascal said.

The glory is easy to see. We tell jokes, write poems, score goals, make music, make babies, build skyscrapers, cure diseases.

But the garbage is easy to see too. We break promises, tell lies. We murder, exploit, cheat, and abuse.

With the same hands, we create wonder AND cause unimaginable pain.

It's like there's a cocktail of glory and garbage shaken up together inside each one of us.

So here's the question: *Why are we like this?*

The first book of the Bible, Genesis, helps us understand both the glory and the garbage.

First, the glory. We're glorious because we've been made by a glorious God.

The word "good" is used seven times in Genesis chapter 1. It's used to describe everything that the Maker makes, including you and me. This God – and the world he creates – is overwhelmingly good.

At the end of the chapter, it says, *"God saw all that he had made, and it was very good"* (Genesis 1:31). A God who lacked generosity or kindness or creativity or beauty could never create something like the perfect universe we see here in Genesis chapter 1.

God creates and sustains life; he puts the first human beings in charge of the rest of creation; he tells them to increase and be fruitful. God gifts them the world. It's an amazing thing. He gifts them the world!

But the word "good" is also used in the Bible when someone finds someone or something lovely.

So when God looks at all creation, and especially at the human beings he's made, he says it's "very good". He's saying that he finds them lovely, captivating, beautiful.

It's not a stretch to say that the relationship between God and humanity begins with love at first sight. God loves his creation, and here at the beginning he looks at it – and those he's made – and he says, *You're glorious. I delight in you.*

One God, but with three distinct "Persons".

As you read the Bible, these three Persons are described as Father, and Son, and Spirit. And they relate to each other in perfect, joyful love.

This is what it means when the Bible says "God is love". It's not just something God does. It's something God is. Before anything existed, he loved.

And the really stunning thing is that he could have kept this perfect love and happiness to himself. Unlike you and me, unlike other gods, he didn't need anything or anyone else so that he could love and be loved. He had that in himself. He didn't need to create anything.

But he did. Because he wants to share the perfect love and happiness he has in himself. He wants to draw others into it.

He wants us to have it too. It's an amazing thing.

And that's why he makes us "in his image". You see that phrase in Genesis 1. Being made in his image means that we're capable of knowing him, loving him and enjoying him.

Just think of the best gift you've ever been given. Now, however good that gift was, hopefully you know that it wasn't as amazing as the human being who gave it to you.

In the same way, we may think that the greatest gift we have in our life is family or sex or sport or beauty or friendship or health or achievement.

But wonderful though these gifts are, they can never be as wonderful as the Giver of those gifts, or the Maker of those gifts. That's why the very greatest pleasure in life isn't enjoying the gifts God has given, wonderful though they are. The greatest pleasure the universe has to offer is enjoying the Giver of those gifts, God himself.

What I mean by "enjoying God" is enjoying his presence, his personality, his perfections. Savouring him, treasuring him, revelling in him, just enjoying who he is, the way that you might enjoy getting to know the very best friend you have. Except of course, the pleasure of enjoying

God himself is infinitely greater than that. Infinitely greater.

Now, maybe this sounds as alien to you as it did to me. I certainly didn't know this as a younger man. The "God" I thought people were talking about made me so bored that occasionally, when I went to church, I used to pass the time by counting the bricks up the wall.

But that's the reality being held out to us in the Bible. Your purpose in life, as a human being made in God's image, is to share in his perfect happiness. There's no happiness on earth that comes close. The greatest gift God can give you is himself.

Being made in God's image also means that we were made literally to "image" him, to reflect him.

Not far from where I live there's a building called the Banqueting House. It was built in the 17th century, and when you go inside, there's this stunning painting on the ceiling.

And the kind people at the Banqueting House realized that the problem with staring up at this beautiful painting on the ceiling is that it quite literally gives you a pain in the neck. You stare at this painting, and after a while it really starts to hurt.

So what they've done to help you admire the painting properly is to put mirrors on the top of trolleys. And you push these trolleys around – you look into the mirror on top of the trolley – and the mirrors enable you to enjoy this glorious painting to your heart's content.

In the same way, like mirrors, you and I were made to reflect God's goodness, his beauty, so the whole world can see it, and share in that happiness too.

And the best thing is, because he's a joyful God, we reflect him best when we enjoy him most. So God wants us to enjoy him!

Now this was such a revelation to me as I got to grips with the Bible. I'd always assumed God wanted me to sing hymns I couldn't follow, in buildings I didn't like, wearing clothes I couldn't stand.

But God wants us to be happy in him, so that we'll reflect out to the world that he is our greatest joy in life, whatever our circumstances.

And by the way, as Genesis 1 makes clear, we're the only part of the universe that God has created in his image. That means we are uniquely privileged – another sign of God's incredible goodness towards us.

So we're the glory of the universe.

But we're also the garbage.

Imagine you've finished your day trip to the Banqueting House. You walk out with your friends, and someone says, "That was fantastic!" And someone else says, "Yeah, it was fantastic. Those mirrors, they were AMAZING! They were brilliant, those mirrors on the wheels. The mirrors were absolutely fantastic."

And you say, "Well, yeah, the mirrors were good. But they were only good because they reflected the ceiling."

The whole point of the mirrors, the reason they're there, is not to draw attention to themselves or anything else, but to reflect the beauty above.

Our purpose is the same: to enjoy God, reflecting HIM as we do that.

But if we're honest, we know we're not like that.

One early author, Augustine, wrote that we're "curved in on ourselves". We're like mirrors that are supposed to be pointed upwards and outwards, but instead we're bent downwards and inwards.

Rather than enjoying and reflecting our Creator, we enjoy and reflect created things more. To put it another way, you and I have other "gods".

You say, "I don't even believe in God". But the Bible says, actually, all of us worship something or someone. Whatever your heart clings to and relies upon, that's your "god".

You see, as mirrors, we can't reflect nothing. We'll always reflect something, whatever that may be. And we'll reflect whatever we love and trust and enjoy most. Whatever our hearts cling to and rely upon for their security.

The reason why the world we live in is now not the world of Genesis 1 – the reason there's garbage as well as glory – is because our hearts cling to and rely upon created things rather than our Creator.

And when we live like that, it ruins everything.

It's just not what you and I were made for. It's like taking a priceless violin – and using it to hammer in tent-pegs. Which is a tragic use of a violin, and a very poor way to put up a tent.

You and I weren't meant to revel in our own glory – we were meant to enjoy an infinitely greater one.

We were meant to enjoy and appreciate and savour and participate in and reflect the infinite goodness and happiness of God himself.

We're far too easily pleased. Why put up with our tiny drops of happiness, when we're made to experience whole oceans of it?

Blaise Pascal said, "Everyone seeks happiness ... without exception."

But are you searching in the right place?

Session 2: Hotel

What would it take for you to trust someone?

Trust that they love you. Trust that they're completely committed to you.

And what would it take for that trust to be broken?

The author A.W. Tozer said, "What comes into our minds when we think about God is the most important thing about us".

Like any relationship, what we think about God, positive or negative, determines whether we want to know him or not.

So when someone says, "I don't believe in God", my question is, "Which God don't you believe in?"

What if the God that we don't believe in, or the God we don't trust, isn't actually the real God, the God of the Bible?

And if you knew that knowing this God would make you happier than anyone or anything else, wouldn't you want to meet him?

What we see in Genesis is that God gives Adam and Eve life and breath and everything they need to flourish. They're free, they're fulfilled, they're secure, they're blissfully happy, and they lack nothing.

You see, this is a God who gives them an entire paradise of "yes", and just a single tree of "no". All he asks is that they trust him.

He says, "You are free to eat from any tree in the garden; but you must not eat from the tree of the knowledge of good and evil…" (Genesis 2:16-17).

A paradise of "yes"; a single tree of "no".

But why would eating from that tree be so significant?

Well, because sometimes small gestures mean something much bigger. Like imagine if someone takes off their wedding ring and just hurls it into the sea. They're just throwing away a tiny piece of metal, right? No big deal. But what it represents is huge. The effects, relationally, would be deep and damaging.

It would be like that with eating from this tree. Like a loving Father to his child, God's saying, *Adam. Eve. I love you. I built this paradise for you. But for this paradise to remain a paradise, you have to TRUST me to be God. Trust me that I know what's best for your happiness.*

If you eat from this tree, you would be saying to me, "I don't trust you. I know better than you what's best for me." You know, you'd be saying, "I can do better. Get out of my life."

So God's saying, *If you choose independence from me, ultimately there's nothing there for you. Please trust me on this. There is no greater happiness apart from me. It doesn't exist.*

The author C S Lewis said that all of history has been "the long, terrible story of mankind trying to find something other than God which will make him happy".

And this moment in Genesis chapter 3, this moment in the shadow of this tree – this is ground zero.

Now yes, of course we've got questions about talking serpents. But this is about us: this is about Adam and Eve, you and I. It's about what comes into our minds when we think about God.

So the serpent says, *"Did God REALLY say, 'You must not eat from ANY tree in the garden'?"* (Genesis 3:1).

Now, of course, God didn't say that. It's a paradise of "yes", and a SINGLE tree of "no".

But you hear what the serpent's saying: *God is mean-spirited. He wants to keep you down. He doesn't want you to be happy. He's keeping the best things from you. Why trust him?*

And then the serpent says, "You will NOT certainly die…" *if you eat from the tree.*

He's saying there are no consequences if you ignore what God has said. It won't hurt you. There's no judgment. In fact, if you eat from the tree, *"your eyes will be opened, and you will be like God"* (Genesis 3:5).

I mean, it has such a familiar ring to it, doesn't it? God is not great. He is not trustworthy. He wants to repress you and ruin your life. He doesn't want your happiness.

And I wonder if that's what comes into your mind when you think about God. Not as the great *source* of happiness, but as the great *spoiler* of happiness.

When we start thinking about God as not trustworthy, not wanting us to be happy, then of course we won't listen to him or love him.

But for many of us, the God we've rejected, or the God we feel has rejected us, is actually not the God revealed here in the Bible. Is it possible we've believed lies about him – the same ones that the serpent tells here?

And think of it from God's perspective. What would it feel like if someone you love – love to the bottom of your heart – what if someone you loved believed lies about you? And what if, because of those lies, they pushed you away?

But Adam and Eve's motivation for pushing God away goes deeper. The reason that they don't trust God isn't just because they lack facts about him. It's not simply that they've been lied to.

The reason they choose not to trust God is because they trust something else for their happiness instead. The Bible says you and I push God away because we've replaced him with something, or someone else, that we think is better, more attractive than God.

And we see exactly what it is in Genesis chapter 3. The serpent says, *"When you eat from [the tree] your eyes will be opened, and you will be like God"* (Genesis 3:5).

See, most of us think that being like God will make us happier than trusting God. Right?

Because of that, we want to "de-God" God, if I can put it that way. We want to make our own rules because we think that'll work out better for us.

And this is one of the central threads of the whole Bible. Will human beings trust their Creator, or will they give their hearts away to someone or something else instead? Will they recognize that God is God, and be happy in that, or will they try to find greater happiness elsewhere?

And this, by the way, is what the Bible means when it talks about "sin".

"Sin" is putting anything or anyone in God's place. When something or someone else becomes more desirable to us than the One who made us, sustains us, and gives us every good thing we enjoy – that is "sin".

Someone put it like this: "The essence of sin is not so much that we want bad things. It's that we want things too badly."

God warns that sin always damages us and others, often in unforeseen ways, and in the end, sin leads to death and judgment.

And that's why the first two of God's Ten Commandments warn us so strongly against putting other gods in his place.

But Adam and Eve make their choice. They trust the serpent rather than God. They bite down on the fruit.

Like a fish going for a baited hook, they don't realize how deadly it is until it's too late.

And like most sin, just for a moment, it tastes really good. Genesis says that as soon as they eat it, "the eyes of both of them were opened" (Genesis 3:7).

But what are their eyes opened to?

Not a happier life, as they'd hoped, but a crippling sense of shame. It says that suddenly, "they realized that they were naked".

Now this isn't just being aware of physical nakedness; it goes much deeper than that.

They feel morally naked. They're ashamed of what they've done. They know they're guilty, but they don't want to admit it,

and so they do what guilty people do. They try to hide themselves. They try to cover up.

And, well, we've been doing the same ever since. How often we hide behind appearances: the status we have, the money we earn, conspicuous consumption, conspicuous religiosity, the faked-out smiles of social media… We do it because, without them, we feel naked.

But then. There is something just so beautiful here in this chapter.

How does God respond to what they've done? It says, *"The Lord God called to the man"* (Genesis 3:9). You see, he comes after him.

God's saying, *Look, come on, you can't hide from me. You can't cover up the truth about yourselves. I know everything you've done. I know everything you are.*

But still I want you. Still I'm coming for you. I'm calling out to you. And I'm going to clothe you and I'm going to provide for you.

Yes, of course there is anger at what Adam and Eve have done. There is a price to be paid for treating their Creator in that way – a price that we've been paying ever since.

He says, from this point on, there'll be pain and conflict between the sexes. Work will be hard and exhausting. Suffering will enter the world. There's banishment from the sweet intimacy they'd once enjoyed with their Creator.

And this, by the way, is why the world we live in now is such a bewildering cocktail of glory and garbage. We're made in God's image, but now, to use the Bible's phrase, we're also "in Adam". We bear HIS family likeness.

And yes, the serpent WAS lying. There IS a price to pay for sin. One day, they will both die. And so will all of those who are "in Adam", including you and me.

But... but...

In the shadow of the tree, something wonderful happens. God's words of judgment are mixed with words of love.

He promises that humanity will continue – Eve will become "the mother of all the living" (Genesis 3:20).

And then, as if he's tenderly embracing them, God provides clothing for them. And the way he does that is really significant. An animal is sacrificed so that they can be clothed.

What if this is an anticipation of some greater sacrifice to come, that would protect them in some greater way?

But most remarkably of all, God promises that the offspring of Eve will at some point in the future "crush [the serpent's] head".

In other words, someone will one day deal with all the garbage, and restore the glory. He'll undo the death and dysfunction. He'll open the way for human beings to return, to run back into the arms of the loving God who made them.

But that is not the end of the sentence. "He will crush [the serpent's] head, and [the serpent] will strike his heel" (Genesis 3:15).

It's an image of being painfully and fatally struck down. So this person will only be able to achieve all this at a terrible cost to himself.

This person – they will defeat death, but in the process, he will himself be killed.

God will put an end to suffering, but only by suffering himself.

You see how different this God is to the one we often have in our minds? How different to every other god you could name? He isn't detached or uncaring. He takes our pain and sorrow with such deadly seriousness that he promises here to enter into it himself.

And so, as God meets Adam and Eve in the shadow of this tree, yes, there is judgment. He can't just pretend that sin doesn't matter, sweeping it under the carpet like a corrupt government official. To tolerate evil is not to be loving; it's the opposite. Sin MUST be punished if God is to be just.

But at the same time there is unexpected, undeserved, unimaginable love. Love that is prepared to go to extraordinary lengths for the sake of the beloved.

What comes into our mind when we think about God is really important. But much MORE important is what comes into God's mind when he thinks about us.

And what comes into his mind is love – love we really don't deserve. God so loves the world that he will one day meet humanity again in the shadow of another tree: a wooden cross.

And once again, rightful judgment will be mixed with extraordinary love.

So, what would it take for you to trust God?

Trust that he loves you?

Trust that he's completely committed to you?

Would you trust God if he were to call out to you in love, just as he called out to Adam and Eve?

Would you trust him if he were to become human, and then, on your behalf, live out the sinless life that you and I find it impossible to live?

Would you trust him if he were to clothe you in such a way that you no longer felt you needed to hide, either from him, or from other people?

Would you trust him if he took the punishment you deserve, in your place?

Would you trust him if, in love, he gave up his life for you?

Session 3: Gold

One of the surprising things I discovered when I got married is that I didn't have to say, "I do" in the ceremony. Neither did my wife. You see, instead, we both had to say, "I will".

Maybe that's just the way that it was in our wedding ceremony and others are different, but we were saying, "I will" because we were making promises to each other.

Our wedding wasn't about stating facts; it was about making promises.

Now, without giving too much away about our marriage, we find that we get into problems when we forget our promises and start making demands. When we forget the times we said, "I will" and we start to say, "You must".

Now, when it comes to God, do you tend to think of him saying, "I will" or "You must"? Is your first thought of God someone who makes promises or someone who makes demands?

Lots of people think of the God of the Bible as being demanding. Like some lonely dictator in the sky, demanding to be obeyed. Looking for perfection, but watching to see you fail.

But, what if I told you that the God of the Bible is not like that at all?

What if I told you that, rather than being demanding, the God who is Father, Son and Spirit is overwhelmingly generous?

Maybe you're thinking about those commandments in the Bible – they sound pretty demanding. Thou shalt not commit murder. Thou shalt not steal...

Well, aside from the fact that you probably agree that stealing and murdering are bad ideas, there's something else we need to understand first. Before God gave those commands, he made promises.

In Genesis, the first book of the Bible – over 400 years before the commandments in the second book – God makes promises to a man named Abraham.

In seven verses, God says, "I will" seven times.

It's like the complete opposite of that JFK quote: as though the God of the Bible is saying to Abraham, *Ask not what you can do for your God but listen to what your God will do for you.*

Now we might think it's pretty irrelevant that God should make promises about land and a large family to some guy who lived in the Persian Gulf around 4,000 years ago. But the outcome of those promises was that *"all peoples on earth will be blessed"* (Genesis 12:3).

Basically, God was promising that one day he would solve all the world's problems through one of Abraham's descendants.

Now that doesn't mean that every single person will be reconciled to God in the end, but it does mean that the God of the Bible is drawing to himself a multi-ethnic, multi-racial group from different social classes and

backgrounds. And all of them through one of Abraham's direct descendants.

This is another wonderful thing about the God of the Bible: he doesn't choose who to bless based on where people have come from, or what they've done, or what they look like. In fact it's almost like he picks the least likely. Because if you're planning to build a whole nation from one man, Abraham seems like a really bad choice.

The Bible gives us little background on Abraham. But we do discover that he's married; his wife's name is Sarah, and she's infertile. And by the time God spoke to him, Abraham was 75 and Sarah was in her 60s.

Now why would God choose this man whose wife can't have children and she's long past the menopause?

The reason – and the Bible shows this again and again – is that God wants us to be absolutely clear about something. He wants us to know that his promises don't depend on human effort, human ability or human possibility. His promise to make Abraham "the father of many" doesn't depend upon Abraham's wife being able to conceive.

God wants us to know that his promises are only fulfilled because of his goodness, his love and his power. Because HE gives – not because of anything we do.

He wants us to understand that he's completely in control in every circumstance. So he promises to do something which is, humanly speaking, impossible.

So the God of the Bible looks to give rather than take. To make promises, not demands.

But a lot of the other "gods" we live for, – the things that drive us – well, they are incredibly demanding and they want to take everything.

If we're driven by a great desire for wealth, for example – if we think that having more money will make us happy – then we'll soon discover that money is a ruthless god.

That might sound ridiculous. How could "wanting more money" be demanding?!

Well, money makes promises. It promises more relaxing holidays, a more secure future, more power, influence and choice. It promises the "good life".

But you're the one who has to do all the work to make that happen. Money doesn't lift a finger to help. It makes the promise but then it demands that you make it happen.

In fact, money drives you mercilessly because even when you think you've made it, you never have quite enough. Living for wealth is exhausting.

When it comes to these gods, their promises only come true if you work hard enough.

But Abraham and Sarah, having been promised something by the God of the Bible, after a while they start to get impatient. It's as though they start to doubt whether God was going to give something to them or demand something from them.

Years pass and there are no children to be seen. So they try to take things into their own hands. In their impatience, and their lack of trust in God's generosity, Abraham gets Sarah's maid Hagar pregnant, and a baby boy is born called Ishmael.

They were working on the assumption that, just like with the other "gods", this promise contained a demand. When God said, "I will", they heard "You must". That's a big mistake to make.

And when we refuse to trust that God is the generous God, and we think of him as demanding instead, it starts a chain reaction of pride, envy, hostility because demanding gods make demanding people.

This is exactly what happens with Abraham and Sarah. Even though it's Sarah's idea for Abraham to sleep with Hagar, she quickly feels animosity towards her once Hagar is pregnant.

When we "worship" these demanding idols, our pride kicks in and we look to compare ourselves with others.

How well do they succeed at meeting the demands of the gods?

If they're doing better than we are, we're envious. If they're less successful than us we become conceited. Either way, other people's "success" in life becomes the standard by which we measure our own.

And of course we tend to look charitably on our own circumstances but find ourselves less generous towards other people and theirs. So, like a child takes after their parents, we become like the gods we worship.

Demanding gods make demanding people.

But what if we worship a generous God?

Well, it means we appreciate what we have as a gift and not an obligation.

Let me explain. If we have to work hard for everything – or at least we think we do – then bizarrely we become entitled. Very quickly we think we're owed something. Because our relationship with these gods is a trade-off – blessings in exchange for work – every exertion of effort, however small, must be rewarded.

So we tend to look very carefully at our "pay cheque". Are these gods paying us enough? And more often than not, we feel cheated or out of pocket.

But when we have a generous God, a God who gives freely, we can consider ourselves blessed. This is how Sarah feels when God gives her a son. In fact she calls him Isaac, which means "laughter", because she's so happy about the gift God has given her.

Now, people don't tend to laugh when they collect their pay cheques. You see, the demanding gods make people joyless. But a generous God, the giving God, the God of the Bible – well, he can make us smile.

So, who is this offspring of Abraham, through whom God would bless all na-

tions? Who's the descendant who would solve the world's problems?

It's Jesus Christ. He is the promise come true.

He's the one who said to all those who are exhausted by the demands of their gods… he says, *"Come to me, all you who are weary and [heavy laden], and I will give you rest"* (Matthew 11:28).

He's the one who says to those who are sick and tired of being minions, *"[I've] not come to be served, but to serve."* (Mark 10:45)

He's the one who washed his disciples' feet.

He's the one who gave his life for people of all nations.

He's the one of whom it was said, *"The wages of sin is death, but the gift of God is eternal life in Christ Jesus our Lord."* (Romans 6:23)

He is the Generous God.

Session 4: Lawn

Hardly any of us think of ourselves as slaves. And yet Jesus says, "Everyone who sins is a slave to sin" (John 8:34).

In the Bible, "sin" is swapping God for anything that's not God. We put someone or something else at the centre of our lives, instead of our loving Creator.

We live for it, love it, devote our energy towards it, spend most of our money on it, make sacrifices for it, daydream about it.

And Jesus says, actually, you're enslaved to it.

"Really?" we say. "I'm not a slave. I'm free to live how I want."

But how free are we, really? How free are we?

For example, all of us instinctively know we ought to treat others in a way we'd want to be treated ourselves. But let me challenge you to live a single day like that. Without any unkindness, or impatience, or lack of generosity.

You see, sin is something we keep doing, even when we know it's wrong, even when we know it's damaging ourselves and others. It's like we can't help ourselves. We're enslaved to it.

Even Paul, the writer of half the New Testament, says, *"I have the desire to do what is good, but I cannot carry it out. For I do not do the good I want to do, but the evil I do not want to do – this I keep on doing"* (Romans 7:18-19).

Jesus said it's because we're slaves to sin.

Is there any way we can be free? That's the question: is there any way that we can be free?

In the book of Exodus, you can read about how the Israelites were enslaved in Egypt.

They'd become numerous and the Egyptians were scared they'd rise up to rebel.

So they were made to work as slaves by Pharaoh, the Egyptian king. Exodus chapter 1 says that the Egyptians "made their lives bitter with harsh labour in brick and mortar and with all kinds of work in the fields; in all their harsh labour, the Egyptians worked them ruthlessly" (Exodus 1:14).

This went on for 400 years. Whole generations who knew nothing except birth, slavery, and death. To weaken them further, Pharaoh ordered that all Israelite baby boys should be killed – thrown into the River Nile.

But God intervenes. He hears their cries for help; his heart goes out to them.

God sends his people a leader, a man called Moses, and tells him to go to the Egyptian king and demand their freedom.

But Pharaoh refuses to listen to him. He punishes the Israelites by making their slavery even harder, even more desperate.

In response, God sends a series of plagues on Egypt, to make Pharaoh release the Israelites.

And here's the shocking thing. Each time Pharaoh promises to release them from slavery. But each time – despite the terrible plagues that are ruining him and his land – each time, Pharaoh goes back on his word. And so another plague comes.

It seems crazy. Why does he keep doing it? Because the Israelites are not the only ones in chains here. Pharaoh's in chains too. He's in slavery to his sin.

Like us, he keeps doing it, even when he knows it's wrong, even when he knows it's damaging to himself and to others.

It's like an addiction. The more he does it, the harder it becomes for him to stop.

And this is a picture of how our sin affects us.

Like Pharaoh, we think that sin is something we're free to choose – that we can walk away from it whenever we want.

But when we try to walk away, we find we can't.

We try to live a single day treating others the way we want to be treated ourselves. We find we can't do it.

We try to stop looking at internet pornography. We find we can't do it.

We try to be more patient with our children, or with someone at work, and we find we can't do it.

Nobody thinks they're a slave – until they start trying to get the chains off.

You see, sin isn't just something we do. After a while, sin starts to "do" us. That's what the Bible means when it says that Pharaoh's heart became "hardened".

The more we sin, the more we become de-sensitized to it.

It seems as if nothing can free the Israelites. Nine plagues have come and gone, but Pharaoh keeps resisting.

So God says, *"I will bring one more plague … on Egypt. After that, [Pharaoh] will let you go"* (Exodus 11:1).

God wants us to understand that nothing less than what's about to happen can break the power of sin, and set people free.

Because Pharaoh refuses to release his people from slavery, God warns them that the firstborn son in every family will die.

But there's a way to avoid this judgment. God tells each Israelite family to slaughter a lamb, and daub some of the blood from the lamb on the top and the sides of the doorframe of their house.

He says, *When I see the sign of the blood on your house, I'll 'pass over' you. Nothing will harm you.*

You see what's happening? The death of the lamb is a stand-in – a substitute for the death of the firstborn son. The lamb dies so they don't have to. The lamb takes the judgment that they would otherwise face, so that they can go free.

So the plague falls as promised. In every house that didn't have blood on the doorframe, the eldest son dies. As a result, Pharaoh tells them that they can leave.

God's people were 400 years in slavery. Finally, 600,000 men, plus women and children, were free.

Saved by a slaughtered lamb.

Some of us think, "Really? A farmyard animal? Deals with the judgment that sin deserves?"

And of course the answer is, no, of course not. The sacrifice of the Passover lamb was a sign, pointing forward to a much greater sacrifice. A greater lamb was coming.

And a much greater liberation.

Fast forward to the time of Jesus, about 1500 years later. A man called John the Baptist sees Jesus, and says, *"Look, the LAMB of GOD, who takes away the sin of the world!"* (John 1:29)

What did he mean? He meant, *Here's the greater lamb, the better lamb, the lamb of GOD.* The one who would deal not merely with literal, physical slavery but a much deeper slavery: our slavery to sin.

Because although God freed the Israelites from slavery in Egypt, like us they weren't free of their slavery to sin.

They needed a greater lamb to deliver them from that. So do we.

You can see that they're still enslaved because, though physically they've left Egypt, amazingly their hearts are still back there. God provides food for them to eat, but then they say, *"If only we had meat to eat!"* *"We were better off in Egypt!"* *"Why did we ever leave Egypt?"* If only things were the way they used to be.

And we're the same. Those two words "if only" also reveal where our hearts really are – who our god really is. Those two words "if only" reveal your Pharaoh. The one who works you ruthlessly and without mercy.

What's your "if only"?

If only I were married. If only I had more respect from people around me. If only I had more money or more leisure time. If only I had better health.

Again and again, like Pharaoh, these things promise to set us free. And like Pharaoh, again and again, they go back on their promise. And we continue to be enslaved by "if only".

As the old song goes, "You're gonna have to serve somebody". And if that somebody or something is anything other than God, it'll keep you in chains.

Some people think that submitting their life to any god would feel like slavery.

But it depends who your god is.

If your god is merciless, ruthless, insatiable for power, always demanding that you work harder and harder, make more sacrifices, then of course you'll be miserable.

But what if, rather than demanding sacrifices, your God sacrifices himself for you? What if your God is merciful, kind, gentle? What if he offers to bear your burdens for you? What if your God fully empathizes with you, understands the temptations you face? What if your God chose to lay down his power, his freedom, his life, in order to serve you?

Back in the day, a ransom price was the price you paid to set a slave free. And Jesus Christ, God the Son, said he gave his life "as a ransom for many" (Mark 10:45).

The original Passover lamb was sacrificed to free God's people from slavery in Egypt. But Jesus is the better Passover Lamb, who sacrifices himself to free us from our slavery to sin.

When you look at Jesus' life and death, you see what kind of God he is. His power was extraordinary, but he never used it to abuse or exploit others. He used it to serve them.

And when you see that, your "if only" is transformed. Your "if only" becomes, "If only I could serve Christ better, and serve others as well as he did. If only I could become more like him." All you want to do in life is use your freedom to serve him.

And when you do that, it feels like true freedom. Because you're not serving your own personal Pharaoh. You're serving a liberating God who gives everything to set his people free.

Jesus said, *"Come to me, all you who are weary and burdened, and I will give you rest ... For my yoke is easy and my burden is light"* (Matthew 11:28-30).

He said, *"[I have come] to proclaim freedom for the prisoners ... to set the oppressed free"* (Luke 4:18).

He said, *[If you follow me,] you will know the truth, and the truth will set you free"* (John 8:32).

He said, *"Everyone who sins is a slave to sin... [but] if [I set] you free, you will be free indeed"* (John 8:34-36).

Session 5: Geisha

In the West, we are richer than we've ever been.

We have more leisure time. More opportunities. More freedom.

And at the same time we have more divorce, more depression, more burnout, more stress-related illness, more suicide.

In other words, more of everything, except fulfilment.

What's going on?

We actually find the answer in an Old Testament book called Jeremiah. It was written in the 7th century BC, and it is a remarkable description of the relationship between God and the ancient people of Israel.

Israel is described as God's "bride", with God as her devoted husband. He loves her with all of his heart, and she loves him devotedly. She trusts him, and she follows him.

God says, *"I remember the devotion of your youth, how as a bride you loved me and followed me through the wilderness"* (Jeremiah 2:2).

That's a picture of what happened when God led his people out of slavery in Egypt. He led them towards a new home, a beautiful new land where they would be free, free to enjoy him forever. And he provided food and water for them as they travelled through the wilderness.

But then, something devastating happens.

God's people abandon God and they chase after other gods instead. To use the language of the Bible, God's bride commits idolatry, an act of spiritual adultery.

And this isn't just a one-off – a momentary lapse. It happens repeatedly.

He loves like a faithful husband, but again and again, God's people give their love to other things instead. They seek satisfaction elsewhere.

The language in Jeremiah is devastating. God says, *"You have lived as a prostitute with many lovers"* (Jeremiah 3:1).

In fact, God's people are shown as worse than a prostitute. A prostitute, after all, is paid for what she does. But God's people went after things which didn't pay.

God says, *"My people have committed two sins: They have forsaken me, the spring of living water, and have dug their own cisterns, broken cisterns that cannot hold water"* (Jeremiah 2:13).

In other words, the things that they traded in for God – the things that they'd exchanged instead of him – they could not bring fulfilment.

And it is a senseless, shocking betrayal of the One who loved them so faithfully.

But actually, even more of a shock is the realization that this is also a picture of us.

We could be, should be, enjoying the source of all fulfilment. But we don't trust him, and so we seek fulfilment elsewhere.

But don't we know from our own experience that, except perhaps for a short time, these things never fill us up?

We get the next pay rise – and pretty soon it's not enough. We get that dream wife or husband – and pretty soon they're not enough. We go after these things expecting so much – and every time we're just disappointed.

There's always the hangover, the morning after. We wake up and we say to ourselves, "This isn't what I hoped it would be". All our dreams come false.

You see, looking to these things to try to fulfil us is like trying to lick up moisture from a dusty, dried-up cistern. They just weren't designed to satisfy in that way. Yet back we go, again and again, to the same broken cisterns.

If we crave lasting fulfilment, we need to go to the source. We need to go to the God who describes himself in Jeremiah as "the spring of living water".

Fast forward 700 years. (You can read about this in John chapter 4.) Jesus sits by a well in a place called Samaria. A Samaritan woman comes to take water from the well.

Now, as a Samaritan, she's a racial and religious outcast. As a woman, she has no power and is looked down on.

Yet Jesus reaches out to her – he asks her for a drink.

And she's shocked. She says to Jesus, *"You are a Jew and I am a Samaritan woman. How can you ask me for a drink?"* (John 4:9)

And Jesus says something staggering. He tells her, *If you understood who I am, you would be asking me for a drink, and I would give you "living water"*. He is identifying himself here with the God who speaks in Jeremiah, who calls himself "the spring of living water".

But the woman misses it – she's still thinking of literal water. She says, *"Sir … you have nothing to draw with and the well is deep. Where can you get this living water?"* (verse 11)

Jesus says, *"Everyone who drinks this water* [the water in the well] *will be thirsty again."*

But then Jesus says this: *"Whoever drinks the water I give them will never thirst. Indeed, the water I give them will become in them a spring of water welling up to eternal life"* (verses 13-14).

You hear what Jesus is holding out to us? An end to the spiritual thirst that's dogged us all our lives – that never-ending quest for fulfilment.

He's saying, *Don't try to be satisfied with broken, dried up cisterns. Career, relationships, material things –they're all good, but they can't quench the deeper thirst. They're gifts from the one who can. Come to the source of all these good things.*

The woman at the well was an outsider, an outcast in every imaginable way.

Because of her beliefs, she was a religious outcast. Because of her race, she was an ethnic outcast. Because of her gender, she was a social outcast. And then we learn something else as well: because of her life choices, she was a moral outcast.

You see, the other women would have come to draw their water early in the day when it was cooler. But the text says this woman came to the well alone at mid-day, when the sun was hottest. Why? Because none of the other women, even the women from her own community, wanted to associate with her.

And Jesus knew why. Without her even having to say so, he knows all about her chequered sexual history. In that culture, to have had three husbands meant that you were written off as an immoral woman. Jesus says, *"I know that you've had five husbands in the past, and the man you're living with now, you're not married to"* (verse 18, our paraphrase).

Now can you see the significance of that? The woman Jesus spoke to at the well was exactly like Jeremiah's description of God's people. A serial adulteress, seeking fulfilment everywhere but in God. Trying to draw water from broken cisterns that can't ultimately satisfy. She is so far from God that even her own people refuse to associate with her.

But how does Jesus relate to her?

With tenderness, with gentleness, with love. He engages with her, he speaks kindly to her, he associates with her. And he crosses all the boundaries we set up for ourselves. And he does all of this so that he can offer her the water that she's really been looking for all of her life.

And if there is hope for her, can't you see, there's hope for all of us?

Imagine one day you switch on the TV, and you see a news report about the royal family. And your jaw drops. In a shocking revelation, the palace confirms that one of the royal princes has married a prostitute.

And then you see her.

She's been living on the streets. She is dealing with a mountain of unpaid debt, so she's homeless, she's dirty, she's hungry and thirsty. There is nothing remotely attractive about her.

And then the cameras cut to an interview with the prince himself. And he says, "I've always loved her. I loved her from the very beginning. And I'll continue to love her. Regardless of who she is and what she's done. Nothing will separate us."

And then the cameras cut away to members of the public. They ask people what they think. And there is uproar. "How on earth can this woman become his wife?" "How could she ever be queen after all she's done?" "It is a disgrace to the entire royal family, not just the prince!"

And of course, in a sense they're right. Because for the prince to marry her, he has to accept the shame connected with her. He has to be willing to associate with her, bind himself to her, be joined to her, pay off the debts she can't pay. He has to pay a huge price.

But that is just a tiny glimpse of what Jesus Christ has done for his people. For people like you and me.

God says that he chose his people before the creation of the world. He loved them faithfully, and he never stopped loving them, even when they betrayed him when they went off after other gods.

On the cross, Jesus Christ associated himself with us, he bound himself to us, he paid off the debts that we can't possibly pay. He took on our shame and disgrace. He paid a huge price.

And not just shame but punishment. All the punishment we deserve for wandering away from God, and looking to broken cisterns for our satisfaction. He willingly took that punishment on himself, on the cross, on our behalf. All so that we could be united to him and be fulfilled in him, forever.

Can you see how much he loves you, and how much that love cost him?

Imagine at the end of the news report, the camera cuts back to the prince. And he looks straight into the camera. And he says, "I know exactly who she is. I know exactly what she's done. But I'm the future king. I marry who I choose to marry. And whatever she may have been, her status changed forever when I married her. Whatever she may have done, she has been welcomed into my family. Everything I have is now hers. I belong to her and she belongs to me. And she will never want for anything again."

And near the end of John's Gospel, John records what Jesus said just before he died on the cross. Jesus cried out on the cross, "I am thirsty" (John 19:28).

The spring of living water himself was thirsty. So that we would never have to be thirsty again.

Session 6: Celebrity

Everybody dies.

And most of us die more than once.

You worship power, and every time you get passed over for promotion or a salary rise, it eats away at you like cancer.

Worship approval, and every time someone ignores you or disagrees with you, it feels like you've been cut to the heart.

Worship comfort, and every imposition on your leisure time feels like life is being taken from you.

Worship control, and when things don't go your way, it makes you so angry you could die.

What, if it was taken from you, would make you feel like life wasn't worth living?

The novelist David Foster Wallace said, "Worship your own body and beauty and sexual allure, and you will always feel ugly, and when time and age start show-ing, you will die a million deaths before they finally plant you".

Do you know that feeling? You know, you're peering into the mirror, and it's like every new wrinkle that appears, every new sag and bag, it's just devastating.

Now of course, it's only your bathroom mirror. But if you start asking it, "Who's the fairest of them all?" it gains the power of life and death over you.

Power. Approval. Comfort. Control. Maybe these "little gods" do make us feel alive, briefly, if we feel we're measuring up. But when we fail them, when we don't measure up, it feels like death.

And that's no illusion. Because finally, after all the little deaths we suffer, we know what's waiting for us in the wings. An actual death, literal and unavoidable.

The book of Romans in the Bible explains why. It says that "the wages of sin is death" (Romans 6:23). In other words, because we've lived for things which are not God, death is our reward, death is our payment.

We earn God's judgment for rejecting him in favour of lifeless things, and ultimately we get the only reward that lifeless things have to offer.

And when we face death ourselves, that's the moment our eyes are opened, and we see just how dead and useless our gods really are. The things we look to when we're in trouble or distress – how effective are they really?

I mean, what good is power, approval, comfort or control when you're lying in a hospital bed, struggling to take a breath?

My first really close encounter with death came in 2001, in a hospice in England, as I watched my mother die of stomach cancer.

She died at the age of 64, on September 15th 2001. And of course 4 days before that, it was 9/11.

And I remember there was a little flickering TV at the end of her bed, so I sat there beside her, watching in disbelief as the twin towers turned to dust right in front of my eyes.

And then, just to my left, as I tried to hold onto her, effectively my own mother was turning to dust with them.

And, I mean, this is a cliché, I'm almost embarrassed to say it. But no one lives forever. Not even the ones you love the most. And not even the ones who love you the most.

Not even the young, the rich and the powerful: those men and women who got up as usual that Tuesday morning to go to work in New York and had no idea that their lives would be over by lunchtime.

These dead gods we live for, they promise us real life, real happiness. But the promise ultimately is shown to be a lie because they cannot deliver us from death.

And that's the litmus test. The litmus test of whether our chosen god is worth living for: does it have an answer to death?

The Gospels tell us that Jesus Christ was tortured and then executed on a cross, in full view of the people of Jerusalem.

And then his corpse was taken down, anointed with spices, it was wrapped in strips of linen and then buried in a tomb. And one of the eyewitnesses of his death shouted up at the cross, *"He saved others … but he can't save himself! … Let him come down now from the cross, and we will believe in him"* (Matthew 27:42).

But Jesus didn't come down from the cross. He died. They thrust a spear deep into his side just to make sure. An expert Roman executioner pronounced him dead. He was buried in a tomb.

So were the religious leaders right? I mean, if someone can't overcome death himself, how can he possibly offer life to anyone else?

But the historical account doesn't end there. Because Jesus didn't end there.

The overwhelming testimony of the Gospels, and the rest of the New Testament, and the explosive growth of those who believed in Jesus, is that death could not keep hold of him.

The Christian churches we see all around us today would not exist were it not for this single historical reality.

In the forty days following his death and burial, Jesus appeared physically not just to his immediate disciples, but to hundreds of people. He spoke with them, he interacted with them, he even ate with them. This was no ghost, no hallucination.

He was physical. He was real. He was tangible and touchable. He was alive.

1 Corinthians chapter 15 says this:

"[Jesus] *was buried ... he was raised on the third day according to the Scriptures, and ... he appeared to* [Peter], *and then to the Twelve* [disciples]. *After that, he appeared to more than five hundred of the brothers and sisters at the same time, most of whom are still living* [in other words, go and talk to them – they'll verify what I'm saying] *... Then he appeared to James, then to all the apostles, and last of all he appeared to me also"* (1 Corinthians 15:4-8).

Now those words were written by a man called Paul. Paul was a hugely respected religious leader who oversaw the execution of Christians.

But then his life was completely up-ended. Because a person he knew was dead actually confronted him. Jesus spoke to him – told him to go into the city, where he'd be told what to do.

Paul became one of the people he'd been persecuting. He spent the rest of his life risking death because he'd seen for himself that Jesus had completely conquered death. And eventually, Paul was executed because he kept insisting Jesus was alive.

Would you willingly give up your life for the sake of something you weren't absolutely sure of?

It makes no sense, unless these early Christians were absolutely convinced that Jesus was fully, physically alive, and

that he'd given them the kind of life that couldn't be ended, not even by public execution on a Roman cross.

Paul said, *"We know that the one who raised the Lord Jesus from the dead will also raise us"* (2 Corinthians 4:14).

What Paul's story shows is that the resurrection isn't just about life after death. It transforms life before death too.

To our remorse for things we've done wrong, even the worst things imaginable, the resurrection says, all of that was paid for by Jesus on the cross, and the price has been accepted.

To all of our regrets, the resurrection says, your best days are ahead of you.

To our anxieties, the resurrection says, don't you see, not even the worst that can happen to you, not even death, can separate you from the life you now have in Jesus.

To our losing a job, or suffering financial problems, the resurrection says, remember: you now have eternal life, that's a treasure that can never be taken from you.

Or to our fretting about getting as much money or attention or as much fun as we can in the here and now, the resurrection says, you don't have to live as if "you only live once", feverishly trying to tick off all the things on your bucket list. You can give your life away for the sake of others, and you'll still have a thousand lifetimes to enjoy in the life to come.

And to our fears in front of the bathroom mirror about getting older, the resurrection says, you are one day closer to a glorious, indestructible body, better than any you've ever known.

If you put your trust in Christ, you are going where he has already gone. You will triumph over death because it will not be able to hold you. Your body will be resurrected, made startlingly new and powerful.

And it won't stop there. The living God doesn't just bring life to our dead bodies. He will bring life to the whole dying world. This world we're living in now will be made new, made right, made perfect. A new creation, filled with new creations.

It's like – the resurrection of Jesus is kind of like – the trailer, the taster, the first visible sign of this coming reality. It's like the first smudge of sunlight on the horizon, proving that the day is coming soon, and cannot be stopped.

In 1 Thessalonians 1, Paul praises those who *"turned to God from idols to serve the living and true God, and to wait for his Son from heaven, whom he raised from the dead – Jesus, who rescues us from the coming wrath"* (1 Thessalonians 1:9-10).

So this leads to a life-or-death question. If worshipping idols leads to death, and brings about God's wrath, well, how can we stop?

We can't just "stop worshipping", because as human beings, we're made to worship. We can't just "stop worshipping" any more than we can just stop eating or just stop breathing.

The only way we can put our idols to death is if we love something else more.

So we need to see the beauty of Christ so clearly that it displaces our love for other gods, so that they lose their hold over us. Jesus must become more desirable to you, more attractive to you, than your idol.

You need to see that he gave up his freedom so that you could be free. He went thirsty so you could be satisfied. He gave up his life so you could live, forever.

The eternal Son of God took on flesh once and for all, took your place once and for all, and took your pain once and for all – suffering on the cross the hell that we deserve, so that we don't have to.

When you see what it means for him not only to die for you, but actually defeat death for you, it just captures your heart as nothing else can. It displaces the idols. Because you realize that no other god has done this for you. No other god could do this for you.

Other gods may promise us eternal life. But only One has proved in history that his promise can be trusted.

You know, the worst feeling I know is waking up and remembering that I've lost something and I can never get it back. A time in my life. A relationship. A mother.

But the promise of the resurrection is not just that I'll be consoled for these losses. The Bible says something much more wonderful. Just listen to this.

It says, *"Our light and momentary troubles are achieving for us an eternal glory that far outweighs them all"* (2 Corinthians 4:17).

That means our worst grief – the things which, looking back, we regret most deeply – are the very things which will make our future resurrection so glorious. And it will be so glorious that we'll happily describe our worst experiences as "light and momentary" by comparison.

If your trust is in Jesus, then not a tear in this life will have been wasted. Every single one of them was preparing in you a greater capacity to enjoy the resurrection that is coming.

Yes, everybody dies. And most of us die more than once.

Because if we love dead gods like power, approval, comfort and control, we'll die a thousand deaths before we actually die.

But if you love the living God, the only one who has defeated death, then you will truly live. After death – and before death too.

Session 7: Space

What is the best gift God could give you?

In 2014, a group of artists and musicians in England asked thousands of people one question and based a show on the answers. The question was: What is your happiest memory?

Well, the answers came in. There were lots of first dates, first dances, first loves. Memories of weddings and births; memories of holidays; the faces of loved ones now lost.

And as they collected these memories of happiness, they noticed three things.

The first was that less than 1% of the happy memories had anything to do with material things. With stuff that could be bought.

Secondly, the memories were nearly always about relationships of one kind or another. Family or friends or lovers.

And they discovered the third thing when they fed all the happy memories into a computer. The word that came up most often was the word "home".

The director said the shows ended up being a cross between a wedding and a wake. It was a celebration mixed with sadness, because these were memories of happiness. The happiness had gone – it hadn't lasted.

What was left was a longing for relationship, and a longing for home.

So why do we have these desires? The author C.S.Lewis said, "If I find in myself desires which nothing in this world can satisfy, the only logical explanation is that I was made for another world".

We were. Open up Revelation chapters 21 and 22, and you'll catch a stunning glimpse of the world you were made for. The reason why our earthly homes and our earthly relationships never fully satisfy. Not even the best ones.

The Bible calls it "a new heaven and a new earth", "the kingdom of heaven", or simply "heaven". A universe of perfect joy, perfect happiness, perfect love.

It's a world where we experience both the ultimate home and the ultimate relationship that deep down we've longed for for all our lives.

Think of it. What is it that makes home so desirable? Comfort? Acceptance? Refreshment? Rest? Being with those we love? Protection from everything that threatens those things?

That's the biblical picture of heaven. All the suffering, rejection, exploitation and loneliness – it's dealt with, removed. Everything sad comes untrue.

All that happened in Genesis 3 is undone. The garbage is dealt with; the glory restored.

But this isn't earth written off and replaced with something completely different. This is the earth renewed, healed, restored. Filled with people who themselves have been renewed, healed, restored. A new creation filled with new creations. Just as real and physical as this creation.

But with no more pain. No more crying. No more injustice. Or unrequited love. Or cruelty. Or concentration camps. Or hospitals. Or hearses. Or separation.

It's a new creation that takes all that is beautiful and joyful in this present life and magnifies it to an infinite degree. Like a book in which each new chapter, each new page, is even more wonderful than the one before.

But heaven isn't just home – the home we've longed for all our lives. It's the relationship we've longed for too.

Read Revelation 21 and 22, and you'll see that at the beating heart of heaven is a wedding.

The love story that began in Genesis 1 reaches its climax. The promise God made to Abraham, that he would draw to himself a multi-ethnic, multi-racial group from every different social class and background, from across every era of history – this is where we see it fulfilled, finally fulfilled.

"I saw the Holy City, the new Jerusalem, coming down out of heaven from God, prepared as a bride beautifully dressed for her husband" (Revelation 21:2).

The Holy City is God's people – a bride perfectly prepared for her husband. After the desperate centuries of tragically giving her heart to other lovers – all the spiritual adultery and idolatry – she is made clean, made beautiful, and drawn into the bridegroom's arms.

And who's the bridegroom, the husband-to-be? Well, the answer comes a few verses later: he's "the Lamb" (verse 9).

"The Lamb" is marrying "the Holy City, Jerusalem".

So that's a fairly unusual wedding, isn't it? I've been at some corkers over the years, but here we've got a troubled Middle-Eastern city being married to a farm-yard animal. Pretty unexpected, even by biblical standards.

But this is a call back to the Passover, when God's people were delivered from slavery in Egypt. The blood of the lamb was put on the tops and the sides of the doorframes so they could escape God's rightful judgment and go free. When God saw the sign of the blood, he "passed over" them. The lamb died so that they don't have to.

That was an anticipation of an infinitely greater liberation, made possible by an infinitely greater Lamb.

So 1500 years later, Jesus Christ – "the Lamb of God", who came to take away the sin of the world – shed his blood on a cross.

All our wrongdoing, all the love we've lavished on created things instead of on our loving Creator… he took the punishment for it. The Lamb died so that we don't have to.

Both the home, and the relationship we've longed for all our lives – they're fully open to us. But only because the Lamb of God, Jesus Christ, died on the cross in our place.

As with any wedding invitation, many are invited, but not everyone comes, and for many different reasons.

That means, as the Bible makes clear, not everyone is included. If heaven is to be heaven, all evil and injustice and wrong-doing must be kept out. That's why, twice in these two chapters, Jesus refers to those who are shut out from the new heaven and the new earth because of their idolatry – all those who have given their lives to worshipping anything or anyone other than Jesus.

Ah, we say, come on. Jesus is the only way in? It's offensive to be so exclusive, so narrow. No one should say that only belief in Jesus will bring us acceptance with God.

But how can there be any other way to God when we look at the cost of entry? If there were any other way, why would the Son of God have to pay in death and blood for our spiritual adultery? It's that serious. Only the cross is uniquely able to pay for it.

The Lamb, the bridegroom, Jesus himself – he died precisely so we would not have to. He took the punishment we deserve, so we wouldn't have to.

Will we accept the invitation to the wedding? Jesus is holding it out to us here.

He wants nothing less than for you to enter into the joy that exists in God himself.

When the French scientist Blaise Pascal died at the age of 39, a small piece of parchment was found sewn into the lining of his coat.

It was his handwritten account of the precise moment when, at the age of 31, he experienced a joy unlike anything he'd known before.

"1654, Monday 23 November… From about half past ten in the evening to about half an hour after midnight…

"FIRE.

"God of Abraham, God of Isaac, God of Jacob, not of philosophers nor of the scholars.

"Certainty. Heartfelt joy. Peace.

"God of Jesus Christ, my God and your God…

"Forgetfulness of the world and of everything, except God…

"Joy, joy, joy.

"Tears of joy."

What was happening to Pascal here?

As he read his Bible, he had encountered Jesus himself. The joyful God. He was experiencing just a tiny foretaste of what heaven will be like. Forgetfulness of the world with all its idols. And in its place: joy.

If we could see into the heart of God, we would see pure, ever-flowing, never-ending joy. The Father joyfully loves his Son. The Son joyfully loves and serves his Father. The Spirit joyfully makes much of the Father and the Son.

Each person of this Trinity – other-focused, self-giving, generously pouring himself out unselfishly for the sake of the others.

It's irrepressible. Overflowing. Like a gushing spring of water. That's why it says here in the final chapter of the Bible, *"Let the one who is thirsty come; and let the one who wishes take the free gift of the water of life"* (Revelation 22:17).

Anyone who tastes this joy, the joy at the heart of God, will never again experience an absence of anything. Complete satisfaction. Complete rest. Complete happiness.

That's the heart of this God – Father, Son, and Spirit – and he is inviting you and me to share in it, to drink from it.

Can you see how staggering this is? No other god is like this God.

That means that the greatest gift God could possibly give you… is himself.

And that is what he does, through his Son Jesus.

What makes heaven heaven is nothing less than being united with God. That's why heaven is described as a place of perfect, unbroken relationship with him:

"God's dwelling-place is now among the people, and he will dwell with them. They will be his people, and God himself will be with them and be their God. 'He will wipe away every tear from their eyes. There will be no more death' or mourning or crying or pain, for the old order of things has passed away" (Revelation 21:3-4).

I remember how I felt when, as a child, I got myself separated from my parents at a huge fair of 20,000 people.

The panic I felt... the awful anxiety... that horrible thought that maybe I'd never see them again. As a five-year-old, I felt the tears starting to burn in my eyes, and my heart breaking. Was I never going to see them again?

But my parents searched for me, and searched for me, and then suddenly I saw them through the crowd. And my mother ran towards me, and swept me up in her arms. And it felt like I'd never loved them as much as I did at that moment. I felt like my heart was going to burst with sheer joy and relief.

Well, that's nothing more than a glimpse of what heaven will be like.

The agony of having been separated from your Father will make the reunion all the more sweet. In that moment, your love for him will be greater than you could ever imagine it to be. Greater than it would have felt had you never been separated. And his love for you – demonstrated by the way he sent his Son to search for you, and find you – will be seen for what it is: the greatest love you've ever known. The greatest joy you've ever experienced.

In a sense, all of history has been "the long terrible story of mankind trying to find something other than God which will make him happy".

We look to sex and relationships, to career, to our homes, our health, our sports, our holidays, to fully satisfy us. But we're far too easily pleased. Even the very best of these things were not designed to bear the weight we try and put on them. When we realize that, we're free to enjoy them for what they are, and nothing more.

That means we won't burden our loved ones with unrealistic expectations that they can fill the hole inside us. It's desperate when people try to do that.

It means we won't expect our occupations or achievements or appearances to save us. We won't expect money to be our saviour.

We were made for another world. One that's never-ending. And that's where our deepest desires will be fully and finally met. In the One who made us to be restless until our hearts find our rest in him.

So let me ask you:

- Is this God the one you live for? If not, which god ARE you living for?

- Did it create you? Does it sustain you? Can it be trusted?

- Does it make big promises, only to leave you disappointed?

- How does it make you feel when you let it down?

- Does it make you feel free, or make you feel enslaved?

- Has it fulfilled you?

- Has it lived like Jesus lived? Loved like Jesus loved?

- Has it laid down its life for you?

- Does it have an answer to death, and has it proved it can deliver on those promises?

• What future does it offer you?

• Is your god as good as this God has shown himself to be?

Revelation chapter 22 makes a promise to all those who love Jesus. It says that in the new heaven and the new earth, "They will see his face" (verse 4).

How many of us have been haunted by the faces of those we've loved. Faces we've lost; faces we've let go; faces that despite our best efforts, couldn't love us in return.

Faces that have either been taken from us by time or circumstance or by death.

But there is a face here in heaven that will satisfy the ache of every broken heart.

And the Bible promises that his people, his bride, will see that face.

The moment you see it, you'll know you've reached your true home.

The moment you see it, you'll know that you've been searching for THIS face in every face you've ever loved.

The best gift God can give you – is himself.

ACKNOWLEDGEMENTS

Life Explored Handbooks

Author   Barry Cooper
Editor   Alison Mitchell
Designer   André Parker

Life Explored Films

Director   Santino Stoner
Producers   Kyle Hill, Corey Petrick
Screenplay   Santino Stoner
Story   Barry Cooper, Nate Morgan Locke,
Corey Petrick, Santino Stoner
Writers   Barry Cooper (Episode 1, 2, 4, 5, 6, 7)
Nate Morgan Locke (Episode 3)
Teachers   Barry Cooper (Episode 2, 6)
Nate Morgan Locke (Episode 3, 5)
Rico Tice (Episode 1, 4, 7)

Special Thanks

To Tim Keller, whose work on idolatry has influenced *Life Explored* in so many ways. In particular, the identification of power, approval, comfort and control as our deepest idols is indebted to Keller.
To Georgia Cooke, Louanne Enns, Reuben Hunter, Ian Roberts and Glen Scrivener.
To All Souls Langham Place, St Bart's Bath, and Trinity West Shepherd's Bush.
To our friends at The Good Book Company.
To those who trialled, those who offered feedback, and those who gave so generously to make *Life Explored* possible.
Life Explored is dedicated with love to Louise Cooper and Cat Morgan Locke.

SUPPORTING
WEBSITE

www.life.explo.red is the official website for *Life Explored*, and features content for both guests and leaders.

Register your course online and you'll receive an exclusive web address where you and your guests can watch any of the films, at any time.

Christianity Explored Ministries (CEM) aims to provide Christian churches and organizations worldwide with resources which explain the Christian faith clearly and relevantly from the Bible. CEM receives royalties from the sale of these resources, but is reliant on donations for the majority of its income. CEM is registered for charitable purposes in both the United Kingdom and the USA. **www.explo.red**